ALSO BY KURT VONNEGUT

Armageddon in Retrospect

And Other New and Unpublished Writings on War and Peace

Kurt Vonnegut

G. P. PUTNAM'S SONS · NEW YORK

PUTNAM

G. P. PUTNAM'S SONS
Publishers Since 1838
Published by the Penguin Group
Penguin Group (USA) Inc., 375 Hudson Street, New York, New York 10014, USA ·
Penguin Group (Canada), 90 Eglinton Avenue East, Suite 700, Toronto, Ontario
M4P 2Y3, Canada (a division of Pearson Canada Inc.) · Penguin Books Ltd, 80 Strand,
London WC2R 0RL, England · Penguin Ireland, 25 St Stephen's Green, Dublin 2,
Ireland (a division of Penguin Books Ltd) · Penguin Group (Australia), 250 Camberwell
Road, Camberwell, Victoria 3124, Australia (a division of Pearson Australia Group
Pty Ltd) · Penguin Books India Pvt Ltd, 11 Community Centre, Panchsheel Park,
New Delhi–110 017, India · Penguin Group (NZ), 67 Apollo Drive, Rosedale,
North Shore 0632, New Zealand (a division of Pearson New Zealand Ltd) ·
Penguin Books (South Africa) (Pty) Ltd, 24 Sturdee Avenue, Rosebank,
Johannesburg 2196, South Africa ·
Penguin Books Ltd, Registered Offices: 80 Strand, London WC2R 0RL, England

ISBN 978-1-60751-143-4

Printed in the United States of America

Book design by Claire Naylon Vaccaro

This is a work containing fiction and nonfiction. Names, characters, places, and incidents,
fictional and factual, are the product of the author's imagination. Any resemblance to actual
persons, living or dead, businesses, companies, events, or locales is entirely coincidental.
The writings by Kurt Vonnegut in this collection have been edited only minimally from
the originals. Typographical and minor factual errors have been corrected.

Contents

Introduction

I trust my writing most and others seem to trust it most when I sound most like a person from Indianapolis, which is what I am.

We might as well have been throwing cream pies.

KURT, ESTIMATING THE NET EFFECT OF THE ANTIWAR
MOVEMENT ON THE COURSE OF THE VIETNAM WAR

Writing was a spiritual exercise for my father, the only thing he really believed in. He wanted to get things right but never thought that his writing was going to have much effect on the course of things. His models were Jonah, Lincoln, Melville, and Twain.

He rewrote and rewrote and rewrote, muttering whatever he had just written over and over, tilting his head back and forth, gesturing with his hands, changing the pitch and rhythm of the words. Then he would pause, thoughtfully rip the barely written-on sheet of typing paper from the typewriter, crumple it up, throw it away, and start over again. It seemed like an odd way for a grown-up to spend his time, but I was just a child who didn't know much.

He had an extra gear language-wise. At eighty-plus he was still doing the *New York Times* crossword puzzles quickly and in ink and never asking for help. As soon as I told him the verb came last, he could translate my Latin homework at sight, without having ever taken Latin. His novels, speeches, short stories, and even dust-jacket comments are very carefully crafted. Anyone who thinks that Kurt's jokes or essays came easily or were written off the cuff hasn't tried to write.

One of his favorite jokes was about a guy who was smuggling wheelbarrows. Every day for years and years a customs agent carefully searched through this guy's wheelbarrow.

Finally, when he was about to retire, the customs agent asked the guy, "We've become friends. I've searched your wheelbarrow every day for many years. What is it you're smuggling?"

"My friend, I am smuggling wheelbarrows."

Kurt would often laugh so hard at his own jokes that he would end up bent in half, looking up with his head in his lap. If it started a coughing fit, it could get a little scary.

When I complained about being paid fifty dollars for an article that had taken me a week to write, he said I should take into account what it would have cost me to take out a two-page ad announcing that I could write.

Anyone who wrote or tried to write was special to Kurt. And he wanted to help. More than once I heard him talking slowly and carefully to drunks who managed to get him on the phone about how to make a story or a joke, the wheelbarrow, work.

"Who was that?"

"I don't know."

When Kurt wrote, he was setting out on a quest. He knew, because it had happened before, that if he could keep the feet moving, he might stumble over something good and work it and work it and make it his own. But as many times as it happened, Kurt didn't have much self-confidence. He worried that every good idea he got might be his last and that any apparent success he had had would dry up and blow away.

He worried that he had skinny legs and wasn't a good tennis player.

He had a hard time letting himself be happy, but couldn't quite hide the glee he got from writing well.

The unhappiest times in his life were those months and sometimes a whole year when he couldn't write, when he was "blocked." He'd try just about anything to get unblocked, but he was very nervous and suspicious about psychiatry.

In my early-to-mid-twenties he let it slip that he was afraid that therapy might make him normal and well adjusted, and that would be the end of his writing. I tried to reassure him that psychiatrists weren't nearly that good.

"If you can't write clearly, you probably don't think nearly as well as you think you do," he told me. If you ever think something he wrote was sloppy, you might be right, but just to be sure, read it again.

A little kid coming of age in Indiana in the Depression decides he wants to be a writer, a famous writer, and that's what ends up happening. What are the odds? He threw a lot of spaghetti up against the wall and developed a keen sense of what was going to stick.

When I was sixteen, he couldn't get a job teaching English at Cape Cod Community College. My mother claimed that she went into bookstores and ordered his books under a false name so the books would at least be in the stores and maybe someone would buy them. Five years later he published *Slaughterhouse-Five* and had a million-dollar multi-book contract. It took some getting used to. Now, for most people looking back, Kurt's being a successful, even famous, writer is an "of course" kind of thing. For me it looks like something that very easily might have not happened.

He often said he had to be a writer because he wasn't good at anything else. He was not good at being an employee.

Back in the mid-1950s, he was employed by *Sports Illustrated*, briefly. He reported to work, was asked to write a short piece on a racehorse that had jumped over a fence and tried to run away. Kurt stared at the blank piece of paper all morning and then typed, "The horse jumped over the fucking fence," and walked out, self-employed again.

I've never known a person less interested in food. The chain-smoking had something to do with it. When he complained about living so long, I told him that God was curious about how many cigarettes a human could smoke and He couldn't help wondering what was going to come out of Kurt's mouth next. The thing that made it hard to take him seriously when he said he was all done and had nothing more to say was that he started saying he was done in his mid-forties and he was still surprising people and coming up with good stuff in his mid-eighties.

The most radical, audacious thing to think is that there might be some point to working hard and thinking hard and reading hard and writing hard and trying to be of service.

He was a writer who believed in the magic of the process—both what it did for him and what it could do for readers. The reader's time and attention were sacred to him. He connected with people on a visceral level because he realized that content was not the whole story. Kurt was and is like a gateway drug or a shoehorn. Once the reader is over the threshold, other writers become accessible.

"Does anyone out of high school still read me?"

.   .   .

He taught how stories were told and taught readers how to read. His writings will continue to do that for a long time. He was and is subversive, but not the way people thought he was. He was the least wild-and-crazy guy I ever knew. No drugs. No fast cars.

He tried always to be on the side of the angels. He didn't think the war in Iraq was going to happen, right up until it did. It broke his heart not because he gave a damn about Iraq but because he loved America and believed that the land and people of Lincoln and Twain would find a way to be right. He believed, like his immigrant forefathers, that America could be a beacon and a paradise.

He couldn't help thinking that all that money we were spending blowing up things and killing people so far away, making people the world over hate and fear us, would have been better spent on public education and libraries. It's hard to imagine that history won't prove him right, if it hasn't already.

Reading and writing are in themselves subversive acts. What they subvert is the notion that things have to be the way they are, that you are alone, that no one has ever felt the way you have. What occurs to people when they read Kurt is that things are much more up for grabs than they thought they were. The world is a slightly different place just because they read a damn book. Imagine that.

Introduction

. . .

It's common knowledge that Kurt was depressed, but as with a lot of things that are common knowledge, there are good reasons to doubt it. He didn't want to be happy and he said a lot of depressing things, but I honestly don't think he was ever depressed.

He was like an extrovert who wanted to be an introvert, a very social guy who wanted to be a loner, a lucky person who would have preferred to be unlucky. An optimist posing as a pessimist, hoping people will take heed. It wasn't until the Iraq War and the end of his life that he became sincerely gloomy.

There was a bizarre, surreal incident when he took too many pills and ended up in a psych hospital, but it never felt like he was in any danger. Within a day he was bouncing around the dayroom playing Ping-Pong and making friends. It seemed like he was doing a not very convincing imitation of someone with mental illness.

The psychiatrist at the hospital told me, "Your dad's depressed. We're going to put him on an antidepressant."

"Okay, but he doesn't seem to have any of the symptoms I'm used to seeing in depression. He's not slowed down, he doesn't look sad, he's still quick on the uptake."

"He did try to kill himself," the psychiatrist said.

"Well, sort of." Of all the medications he took, there wasn't a toxic level of anything. He had a barely therapeutic level of Tylenol.

"Do you not think we should put him on antidepressants? We have to do something."

"I just thought I should mention that he doesn't seem depressed. It's very hard to say what Kurt is. I'm not saying he's well."

The difference between my fans and Kurt's is that my fans know they're mentally ill.

Kurt could pitch better than he could catch. It was routine for him to write and say provocative, not always kind things about people in the family. We learned to get over it. It was just Kurt. But when I mentioned in an article that Kurt, wanting to be a famous pessimist, might have envied Twain and Lincoln their dead children, he went ballistic.

"I was just trying to pull readers in. No one but you is going to take it even a little seriously."

"I know how jokes work."

"So do I."

Click and click, we hung up.

"If I should die, God forbid."

Every few years he sent me a letter telling me what to do in the event of his death. Every time, except the last, the letter would be followed by a phone call, reassuring me that it wasn't a suicide note. The day before he sent me his last "If

I should die" letter, he finished the speech he was to deliver in Indiana to kick off the year of Kurt Vonnegut. Two weeks later he fell, hit his head, and irreversibly scrambled his precious egg.

I got to study that last speech much closer than most, since I was asked to deliver it. I couldn't help wondering, "How on earth does he get away with some of this crap?" His audience made it work. I quickly realized that I was reading his words to an auditorium and a world utterly in love with my father who would have followed him anywhere.

"[I'm] as celibate as fifty percent of the heterosexual Roman Catholic clergy" is a sentence with no meaning. "A twerp [is] a guy who put a set of false teeth up his rear end and bit the buttons off the back seats of taxicabs." "A snarf is someone who sniffs girls' bicycle seats." Where oh where is my dear father going? And then he would say something that cut to the heart of the matter and was outrageous and true, and you believed it partly because he had just been talking about celibacy and twerps and snarfs.

"I wouldn't be a doctor for anything. That's got to be the worst job in the world."

One of our last conversations:
"How old are you, Mark?"
"I'm fifty-nine, Dad."

"That's old."

"Yes it is, Dad."

I loved him dearly.

These writings, mostly undated and all unpublished, hold up very nicely by themselves. They don't need any commentary by me. Even if the content of any given piece isn't interesting to you, look at the structure and rhythm and choices of words. If you can't learn about reading and writing from Kurt, maybe you should be doing something else.

His last words in the last speech he wrote are as good a way as any for him to say good-bye.

And I thank you for your attention, and I'm out of here.

Mark Vonnegut
September 1, 2007

FROM:

Pfc. K. Vonnegut, Jr.,
12102964 U. S. Army.

TO:

Kurt Vonnegut,
Williams Creek,
Indianapolis, Indiana.

Dear people:

I'm told that you were probably never informed that I was anything other than "missing in action." Chances are that you also failed to receive any of the letters I wrote from Germany. That leaves me a lot of explaining to do -- in precis:

I've been a prisoner of war since December 19th, 1944, when our division was cut to ribbons by Hitler's last desperate thrust through Luxemburg and Belgium. Seven Fanatical Panzer Divisions hit us and cut us off from the rest of Hodges' First Army. The other American Divisions on our flanks managed to pull out: We were obliged to stay and fight. Bayonets aren't much good against tanks: Our ammunition, food and medical supplies gave out and our casualties out-numbered those who could still fight - so we gave up. The 106th got a Presidential Citation and some British Decoration from Montgomery for it, I'm told, but I'll be damned if it was worth it. I was one of the few who weren't wounded. For that much thank God.

Well, the supermen marched us, without food, water or sleep to Limberg, a distance of about sixty miles, I think, where we were loaded and locked up, sixty men to each small, unventilated, unheated box car. There were no sanitary accommodations -- the floors were covered with fresh cow dung. There wasn't room for all of us to lie down. Half slept while the other half stood. We spent several days, including Christmas, on that Limberg siding. On Christmas eve the Royal Air Force bombed and strafed our unmarked train. They killed about one-hundred-and-fifty of us. We got a

little water Christmas Day and moved slowly across Germany to a large
P.O.W. Camp in Muhlburg, South of Berlin. We were released from the
box cars on New Year's Day. The Germans herded us through scalding
delousing showers. Many men died from shock in the showers after ten
days of starvation, thirst and exposure. But I didn't.

Under the Geneva Convention, Officers and Non-commissioned
Officers are not obliged to work when taken prisoner. I am, as you
know, a Private. One-hundred-and-fifty such minor beings were
shipped to a Dresden work camp on January 10th. I was their leader
by virtue of the little German I spoke. It was our misfortune to
have sadistic and fanatical guards. We were refused medical attention and clothing: We were given long hours at extremely hard labor.
Our food ration was two-hundred-and-fifty grams of black bread and
one pint of unseasoned potato soup each day. After desperately trying
to improve our situation for two months and having been met with bland
smiles I told the guards just what I was going to do to them when the
Russians came. They beat me up a little. I was fired as group
leader. Beatings were very small time: -- one boy starved to death
and the SS Troops shot two for stealing food.

On about February 14th the Americans came over, followed by the
R.A.F. their combined labors killed 250,000 people in twenty-four
hours and destroyed all of Dresden -- possibly the world's most
beautiful city. But not me.

After that we were put to work carrying corpses from Air-Raid
shelters; women, children, old men; dead from concussion, fire or
suffocation. Civilians cursed us and threw rocks as we carried bodies
to huge funeral pyres in the city.

When General Patton took Leipzig we were evacuated on foot to
Hellexisdorf on the Saxony-Czechoslovakian border. There we remained

until the war ended. Our guards deserted us. On that happy day the
Russians were intent on mopping up isolated outlaw resistance in our
sector. Their planes (P-39's) strafed and bombed us, killing fourteen,
but not me.

Eight of us stole a team and wagon. We traveled and looted our
way through Sudetenland and Saxony for eight days, living like kings.
The Russians are crazy about Americans. The Russians picked us up in
Dresden. We rode from there to the American lines at Halle in Lend-
Lease Ford trucks. We've since been flown to Le Havre.

I'm writing from a Red Cross Club in the Le Havre P.O.W. Repat-
riation Camp. I'm being wonderfully well feed and entertained. The
state-bound ships are jammed, naturally, so I'll have to be patient.
I hope to be home in a month. Once home I'll be given twenty-one days
recuperation at Atterbury, about $600 back pay and -- get this --
sixty (60) days furlough!

I've too damned much to say, the rest will have to wait. I can't
receive mail here so don't write.   May 29, 1945

                              Love,

                                 Kurt - Jr.

Kurt Vonnegut

at Clowes Hall, Indianapolis,

April 27, 2007

Thank you.

I now stand before you as a role model, courtesy of Mayor Bart Peterson, and God bless him for this occasion.

If this isn't nice, I don't know what is.

And just think of this: In only three years' time, during World War Two, I went from Private to Corporal, a rank once held by both Napoleon and Adolf Hitler.

I am actually Kurt Vonnegut, Junior. And that's what my kids, now in late middle age like me, still call me when talking about me behind my back: "Junior this and Junior that."

But whenever you look at the Ayres clock at the Intersection of South Meridian and Washington Streets, please think of my father, Kurt Vonnegut, Senior, who designed it. As far as that goes, he and his father, Bernard Vonnegut, designed the whole darn building. And he was a founder of The Orchard School and The Children's Museum.

. . .

His father, my grandfather the architect Bernard Vonnegut, designed, among other things, The Athenæum, which before the First World War was called "Das Deutsche Haus." I can't imagine why they would have changed the name to "The Athenæum," unless it was to kiss the ass of a bunch of Greek-Americans.

I guess all of you know that I am suing the manufacturer of Pall Mall cigarettes, because their product didn't kill me, and I'm now eighty-four. Listen: I studied anthropology at the University of Chicago after the Second World War, the last one we ever won. And the physical anthropologists, who had studied human skulls going back thousands of years, said we were only supposed to live for thirty-five years or so, because that's how long our teeth lasted without modern dentistry.

Weren't those the good old days: thirty-five years and we were out of here. Talk about intelligent design! Now all the Baby Boomers who can afford dentistry and health insurance, poor bastards, are going to live to be a hundred!

Maybe we should outlaw dentistry. And maybe doctors should quit curing pneumonia, which used to be called "the old people's friend."

. . .

But the last thing I want to do tonight is to depress you. So I have thought of something we can all do tonight which will definitely be upbeat. I think we can come up with a statement on which all Americans, Republican or Democrat, rich or poor, straight or gay, can agree, despite our country's being so tragically and ferociously divided.

The first universal American sentiment I came up with was "Sugar is sweet."

And there is certainly nothing new about a tragically and ferociously divided United States of America, and especially here in my native state of Indiana. When I was a kid here, this state had within its borders the national headquarters of the Ku Klux Klan, and the site of the last lynching of an African-American citizen north of the Mason-Dixon Line, Marion, I think.

But it also had, and still has, in Terre Haute, which now boasts a state-of-the-art lethal-injection facility, the birthplace and home of the labor leader Eugene Debs. He lived from 1855 to 1926, and led a nationwide strike against the railroads. He went to prison for a while because he opposed our entry into World War One.

And he ran for President several times, on the Socialist Party ticket, saying things like this: "While there is a lower class, I am in it; while there is a criminal element, I am of it; and while there is a soul in prison, I am not free."

Debs pretty much stole that from Jesus Christ. But it is so hard to be original. Tell me about it!

But all right, what is a statement on which all Americans can agree? "Sugar is sweet," certainly. But since we are on the property of a university, we can surely come up with something which has more cultural heft. And this is my suggestion: "The Mona Lisa, the picture by Leonardo da Vinci, hanging in the Louvre in Paris, France, is a perfect painting."

OK? A show of hands, please. Can't we all agree on that?

OK, take down your hands. I'd say the vote is unanimous, that the Mona Lisa is a perfect painting. The only trouble with that, which is the trouble with practically everything we believe: It isn't true.

Listen: Her nose is tilted to the right, OK? That means the right side of her face is a receding plane, going away from us. OK? But there is no foreshortening of her features on that side, giving the effect of three dimensions. And Leonardo could so easily have done that foreshortening. He was simply too lazy to do it. And if he were Leonardo da Indianapolis, I would be ashamed of him.

. . .

No wonder she has such a cockeyed smile.

And somebody might now want to ask me, "Can't you ever be serious?" The answer is, "No."

When I was born at Methodist Hospital on November eleventh, 1922, and this city back then was as racially segregated as professional basketball and football teams are today, the obstetrician spanked my little rear end to start my respiration. But did I cry? No.

I said, "A funny thing happened on the way down the birth canal, Doc. A bum came up to me and said he hadn't had a bite for three days. So I bit him!"

But seriously, my fellow Hoosiers, there's good news and bad news tonight. This is the best of times and the worst of times. So what else is new?

The bad news is that the Martians have landed in Manhattan, and have checked in at the Waldorf-Astoria. The good news is that they only eat homeless people of all colors, and they pee gasoline.

Am I religious? I practice a disorganized religion. I belong to an unholy disorder. We call ourselves "Our Lady of Perpetual Consternation." We are as celibate as fifty percent of the heterosexual Roman Catholic clergy.

. . .

Actually—and when I hold up my right hand like this, it means I'm not kidding, that I give my Word of Honor that what I'm about to say is true. So actually, I am honorary President of the American Humanist Society, having succeeded the late, great science fiction writer Isaac Asimov in that utterly functionless capacity. We Humanists behave as well as we can, without any expectation of rewards or punishments in an Afterlife. We serve as best we can the only abstraction with which we have any real familiarity, which is our community.

We don't fear death, and neither should you. You know what Socrates said about death, in Greek, of course? "Death is just one more night."

As a Humanist, I love science. I hate superstition, which could never have given us A-bombs.

I love science, and not only because it has given us the means to trash the planet, and I don't like it here. It has found the answers to two of our biggest questions: How did the Universe begin, and how did we and all other animals get the wonderful bodies we have, with eyes and brains and kidneys and so on?

OK. So science sent the Hubble telescope out into space, so it could capture light and the absence thereof, from the very beginning of time. And the telescope really did that. So now we know that there was once absolutely nothing, such a perfect nothing that there wasn't even nothing or once. Can you imagine that? You can't, because there isn't even nothing to imagine.

But then there was this great big BANG! And that's where all this crap came from.

And how did we get our wonderful lungs and eyebrows and teeth and toenails and assholes and so on? By means of millions of years of natural selection. That's when one animal dies and another one copulates. Survival of the fittest!

But look: If you should kill somebody, whether accidentally or on purpose, improving our species, please don't copulate afterwards. That's what causes babies, in case your mother didn't tell you.

And yes, my fellow Hoosiers, and I have never denied being one of you: This is indeed the Apocalypse, the end of everything, as prophesied by Saint John the Divine and Saint Kurt the Vonnegut.

Even as I speak, the very last polar bear may be dying of hunger on account of climate change, on account of us. And I will sure miss the polar bears. Their babies are so warm and cuddly and trusting, just like ours.

. . .

Does this old poop have any advice for young people in times of such awful trouble? Well, I'm sure you know that our country is the only so-called advanced nation that still has a death penalty. And torture chambers. I mean, why screw around?

But listen: If anyone here should wind up on a gurney in a lethal-injection facility, maybe the one at Terre Haute, here is what your last words should be: "This will certainly teach me a lesson."

If Jesus were alive today, we would kill him with lethal injection. I call that progress. We would have to kill him for the same reason he was killed the first time. His ideas are just too liberal.

My advice to writers just starting out? Don't use semicolons! They are transvestite hermaphrodites, representing exactly nothing. All they do is suggest you might have gone to college.

So first the Mona Lisa, and now semicolons. I might as well clinch my reputation as a world-class nutcase by saying something good about Karl Marx, commonly believed in this country, and surely in Indian-no-place, to have been one of the most evil people who ever lived.

He did invent Communism, which we have long been

taught to hate, because we are so in love with Capitalism, which is what we call the casinos on Wall Street.

Communism is what Karl Marx hoped could be an economic scheme for making industrialized nations take as good care of people, and especially of children and the old and disabled, as tribes and extended families used to do, before they were dispersed by the Industrial Revolution.

And I think maybe we might be wise to stop bad-mouthing Communism so much, not because we think it's a good idea, but because our grandchildren and great-grandchildren are now in hock up to their eyeballs to the Communist Chinese.

And the Chinese Communists also have a big and superbly equipped army, something we don't have. We're too cheap. We just want to nuke everybody.

But there are still plenty of people who will tell you that the most evil thing about Karl Marx was what he said about religion. He said it was the opium of the lower classes, as though he thought religion was bad for people, and he wanted to get rid of it.

But when Marx said that, back in the 1840s, his use of the word "opium" wasn't simply metaphorical. Back then real opium was the only painkiller available, for toothaches or cancer of the throat, or whatever. He himself had used it.

As a sincere friend of the downtrodden, he was saying he

was glad they had something which could ease their pain at least a little bit, which was religion. He liked religion for doing that, and certainly didn't want to abolish it. OK?

He might have said today as I say tonight, "Religion can be Tylenol for a lot of unhappy people, and I'm so glad it works."

About the Chinese Communists: They are obviously much better at business than we are, and maybe a lot smarter, Communists or not. I mean, look how much better they do in our schools over here. Face it! My son, Mark, a pediatrician, was on the Admissions Committee of the Harvard Medical School a while back, and he said that if they had played the admissions game fairly, half of the entering class would be Asian women.

But back to Karl Marx: How subservient to Jesus, or to a humane God Almighty, were the leaders of this country back in the 1840s, when Marx said such a supposedly evil thing about religion? They had made it perfectly legal to own human slaves, and weren't going to let women vote or hold public office, God forbid, for another eighty years.

I got a letter a while back from a man who had been a captive in the American penal system since he was sixteen years old. He is now forty-two, and about to get out. He asked me what he should do. I told him what Karl Marx would have told him: "Join a church."

And now please note that I have raised my right hand. And that means that I'm not kidding, that whatever I say next I believe to be true. So here goes: The most spiritually splendid American phenomenon of my lifetime wasn't our contribution to the defeat of the Nazis, in which I played such a large part, or Ronald Reagan's overthrow of Godless Communism, in Russia at least.

The most spiritually splendid American phenomenon of my lifetime is how African-American citizens have maintained their dignity and self-respect, despite their having been treated by white Americans, both in and out of government, and simply because of their skin color, as though they were contemptible and loathsome, and even diseased.

Their churches have surely helped them to do that. So there's Karl Marx again. There's Jesus again.

And what gift of America to the rest of the world is actually most appreciated by the rest of the world? It is African-American jazz and its offshoots. What is my definition of jazz? "Safe sex of the highest order."

.   .   .

The two greatest Americans of my lifetime, so far as I know, were Franklin Delano Roosevelt and Martin Luther King, Jr.

I have heard it suggested that Roosevelt wouldn't have had such empathy for the lower classes, would have been just another rich, conceited, ruling-class Ivy League horse's ass, if he himself hadn't been humbled by poliomyelitis, infantile paralysis. All of a sudden his legs didn't work anymore.

What can we do about global warming? We could turn out the lights, I guess, but please don't. I can't think of any way to repair the atmosphere. It's way too late. But there is one thing I can fix, and fix this very night, and right here in Indianapolis. It's the name of another good university you've built since my time. But you've named it "I.U.P.U.I." "I.U.P.U.I."? Have you lost your wits?

"Hi, I went to Harvard. Where did you go?"

"I went to I.U.P.U.I."

With the unlimited powers vested in me by Mayor Peterson for the whole year of 2007, I rename I.U.P.U.I. "Tarkington University."

"Hi, I went to Harvard. Where did you go?"

"I went to Tarkington." Ain't that classy?

Done and done.

. . .

With the passage of time, nobody will know or care who Tarkington was. I mean, who nowadays gives a rat's ass who Butler was? This is Clowes Hall, and I actually knew some real Cloweses. Nice people.

But let me tell you: I would not be standing before you tonight if it hadn't been for the example of the life and works of Booth Tarkington, a native of this city. During his time, 1869 to 1946, which overlapped my own time for twenty-four years, Booth Tarkington became a beautifully successful and respected writer of plays, novels, and short stories. His nickname in the literary world, one I would give anything to have, was "The Gentleman from Indiana."

When I was a kid, I wanted to be like him.

We never met. I wouldn't have known what to say. I would have been gaga with hero worship.

Yes, and by the unlimited powers vested in me by Mayor Peterson for this entire year, I demand that somebody here mount a production in Indianapolis of Booth Tarkington's play *Alice Adams*.

By a sweet coincidence, "Alice Adams" was also the married name of my late sister, a six-foot-tall blond bombshell, who is now in Crown Hill along with our parents and grandparents and great-grandparents, and James Whitcomb Riley, the highest-paid American writer of his time.

You know what my sister Allie used to say? She used to

say, "Your parents ruin the first half of your life, and your kids ruin the second half."

James Whitcomb Riley, "The Hoosier Poet," was the highest-paid American writer of his time, 1849 to 1916, because he recited his poetry for money in theaters and lecture halls. That was how delighted by poetry ordinary Americans used to be. Can you imagine?

You want to know something the great French writer Jean-Paul Sartre said one time? He said, in French of course, "Hell is other people." He refused to accept a Nobel Prize. I could never be that rude. I was raised right by our African-American cook, whose name was Ida Young.

During the Great Depression, African-American citizens were heard to say this, along with a lot of other stuff, of course: "Things are so bad white folks got to raise their own kids."

But I wasn't raised right by Ida Young alone, a great-grandchild of slaves, who was intelligent, kind and honorable, proud and literate, articulate and thoughtful and pleasing in appearance. Ida Young loved poetry, and used to read poems to me.

I was also raised right by teachers at School 43, "The James Whitcomb Riley School," and then at Shortridge High School. Back then, great public school teachers were local celebrities. Grateful former students, well into adult life, used to visit them, and tell them how they were doing. And I myself used to be a sentimental adult like that.

But long ago now, all my favorite teachers went the way of most of the polar bears.

The very best thing you can be in life is a teacher, provided that you are crazy in love with what you teach, and that your classes consist of eighteen students or fewer. Classes of eighteen students or fewer are a family, and feel and act like one.

When my grade graduated from School 43, with the Great Depression going on, with almost no business or jobs, and with Hitler taking charge of Germany, each of us had to say in writing what we hoped to do when grown-ups to make this a better world.

I said I would cure cancer with chemicals, while working for Eli Lilly.

I have the humorist Paul Krasner to thank for pointing out a big difference between George W. Bush and Hitler: Hitler was elected.

I mentioned my only son, Mark Vonnegut, a while back. You know: about Chinese women and Harvard Medical School?

Well, he is not only a pediatrician in the Boston area, but a painter and a saxophonist and a writer. He wrote one heck of a good book called *The Eden Express*. It is about his mental crack-up, padded-cell-and-straitjacket stuff. He had been on the wrestling team as an undergraduate in college. Some maniac!

In his book he tells about how he recovered sufficiently to graduate from Harvard Medical School. *The Eden Express*, by Mark Vonnegut.

But don't borrow it. For God's sake, buy it!

I consider anybody who borrows a book instead of buying it, or lends one, a twerp. When I was a student at Shortridge High School a million years ago, a twerp was defined as a guy who put a set of false teeth up his rear end and bit the buttons off the back seats of taxicabs.

But I hasten to say, should some impressionable young person here tonight, at loose ends and from a dysfunctional family, resolve to take a shot at being a real twerp tomorrow, that there are no longer buttons on the back seats of taxicabs. Times change!

I asked Mark a while back what life was all about, since I didn't have a clue. He said, "Dad, we are here to help each other get through this thing, whatever it is." Whatever it is.

· · ·

"Whatever it is." Not bad. That one could be a keeper.

And how should we behave during this Apocalypse? We should be unusually kind to one another, certainly. But we should also stop being so serious. Jokes help a lot. And get a dog, if you don't already have one.

I myself just got a dog, and it's a new crossbreed. It's half French poodle and half Chinese shih tzu.

It's a shit-poo.

And I thank you for your attention, and I'm out of here.

Wailing Shall Be in All Streets

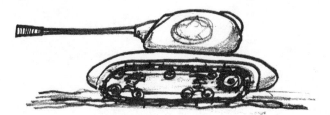

It was a routine speech we got during our first day of basic training, delivered by a wiry little lieutenant: "Men,
up to now you've been good, clean, American boys with an
American's love for sportsmanship and fair play. We're here
to change that. Our job is to make you the meanest, dirtiest
bunch of scrappers in the history of the World. From now
on you can forget the Marquess of Queensberry Rules and
every other set of rules. Anything and everything goes.
Never hit a man above the belt when you can kick him below it. Make the bastard scream. Kill him any way you can.
Kill, kill, kill, do you understand?"

His talk was greeted with nervous laughter and general
agreement that he was right. "Didn't Hitler and Tojo say
the Americans were a bunch of softies? Ha! They'll find
out." And of course, Germany and Japan did find out: a
toughened-up democracy poured forth a scalding fury that
could not be stopped. It was a war of reason against bar-
barism, supposedly, with the issues at stake on such a high

plane that most of our feverish fighters had no idea why they were fighting—other than that the enemy was a bunch of bastards. A new kind of war, with all destruction, all killing approved. Germans would ask, "Why are you Americans fighting us?" "I don't know, but we're sure beating the hell out of you," was a stock answer.

A lot of people relished the idea of total war: it had a modern ring to it, in keeping with our spectacular technology. To them it was like a football game: "Give 'em the axe, the axe, the axe . . ." Three small-town merchants' wives, middle-aged and plump, gave me a ride when I was hitch-hiking home from Camp Atterbury. "Did you kill a lot of them Germans?" asked the driver, making cheerful small-talk. I told her I didn't know. This was taken for modesty. As I was getting out of the car, one of the ladies patted me on the shoulder in motherly fashion: "I'll bet you'd like to get over and kill some of them dirty Japs now, wouldn't you?" We exchanged knowing winks. I didn't tell those simple souls that I had been captured after a week at the front; and more to the point, what I knew and thought about killing dirty Germans, about total war. The reason for my being sick at heart then and now has to do with an incident that received cursory treatment in the American newspapers. In February, 1945, Dresden, Germany, was destroyed, and with it over one hundred thousand human beings. I was there. Not many know how tough America got.

I was among a group of one hundred and fifty infantry privates, captured in the Bulge breakthrough and put to work in Dresden. Dresden, we were told, was the only major German city to have escaped bombing so far. That was in January, 1945. She owed her good fortune to her unwarlike countenance: hospitals, breweries, food-processing plants, surgical supply houses, ceramics, musical instrument factories, and the like. Since the war, hospitals had become her prime concern. Every day hundreds of wounded came into the tranquil sanctuary from the east and west. At night we would hear the dull rumble of distant air raids. "Chemnitz is getting it tonight," we used to say, and speculated what it might be like to be under the yawning bomb-bays and the bright young men with their dials and cross-hairs. "Thank heaven we're in an 'open city,'" we thought, and so thought the thousands of refugees—women, children, and old men— who came in a forlorn stream from the smouldering wreckage of Berlin, Leipzig, Breslau, Munich. . . . They flooded the city to twice its normal population.

There was no war in Dresden. True, planes came over nearly every day and the sirens wailed, but the planes were always en route elsewhere. The alarms furnished a relief period in a tedious work day, a social event, a chance to gossip in the shelters. The shelters, in fact, were not much more than a gesture, casual recognition of the national emergency: wine cellars and basements with benches in them and sand bags blocking the windows, for the most part. There were a few more adequate bunkers in the center of the city, close to the government offices, but nothing like the staunch subterranean fortress that rendered Berlin impervious to her daily pounding. Dresden had no reason to prepare for attack—and thereby hangs a beastly tale.

Dresden was surely among the World's most lovely cities. Her streets were broad, lined with shade-trees. She was sprinkled with countless little parks and statuary. She had marvelous old churches, libraries, museums, theaters, art galleries, beer gardens, a zoo, and a renowned university. It was at one time a tourist's paradise. They would be far better informed on the city's delights than am I. But the impression I have is that in Dresden—in the physical city— were the symbols of the good life; pleasant, honest, intelligent. In the Swastika's shadow those symbols of the dignity and hope of mankind stood waiting, monuments to truth. The accumulated treasure of hundreds of years, Dresden spoke eloquently of those things excellent in European civilization wherein our debt lies deep. I was a prisoner, hungry, dirty, and full of hate for our captors, but I loved that city and saw the blessed wonder of her past and the rich promise of her future.

In February, 1945, American bombers reduced this treasure to crushed stone and embers; disemboweled her with high-explosives and cremated her with incendiaries.

The atom bomb may represent a fabulous advance, but it is interesting to note that primitive TNT and thermite managed to exterminate in one bloody night more people than died in the whole London blitz. Fortress Dresden fired a dozen shots at our airmen. Once back at their bases and sipping hot coffee, they probably remarked, "Flak unusually light tonight. Well, guess it's time to turn in." Captured British pilots from tactical fighter units (covering front-line troops) used to chide those who had flown heavy bombers on city raids with, "How on Earth did you stand the stink of boiling urine and burning perambulators?"

A perfectly routine piece of news: "Last night our planes attacked Dresden. All planes returned safely." The only good German is a dead one: over one hundred thousand evil men, women, and children (the able-bodied were at the fronts) forever purged of their sins against humanity. By chance I met a bombardier who had taken part in the attack. "We hated to do it," he told me.

The night they came over we spent in an underground meat locker in a slaughterhouse. We were lucky, for it was the best shelter in town. Giants stalked the Earth above us. First came the soft murmur of their dancing on the outskirts, then the grumbling of their plodding toward us, and finally the ear-splitting crashes of their heels upon us—and thence to the outskirts again. Back and forth they swept: saturation bombing.

"I screamed and I wept and I clawed the walls of our shelter," an old lady told me. "I prayed to God to 'please, please, please, dear God, stop them.' But he didn't hear me. No power could stop them. On they came, wave after wave. There was no way we could surrender; no way to tell them we couldn't stand it anymore. There was nothing anyone could do but sit and wait for morning." Her daughter and grandson were killed.

Our little prison was burned to the ground. We were to be evacuated to an outlying camp occupied by the South African prisoners. Our guards were a melancholy lot, aged Volkssturmers and disabled veterans. Most of them were Dresden residents and had friends and families somewhere in the holocaust. A corporal, who had lost an eye after two years on the Russian front, ascertained before we marched that his wife, his two children, and both of his parents had been killed. He had one cigarette. He shared it with me.

Our march to new quarters took us on the city's edge. It was impossible to believe that anyone survived in its heart. Ordinarily the day would have been cold, but occasional gusts from the colossal inferno made us sweat. And ordinarily the day would have been clear and bright, but an opaque and towering cloud turned noon to twilight. A grim procession clogged the outbound highways; people with blackened faces streaked with tears, some bearing wounded, some bearing dead. They gathered in the fields. None spoke. A few with Red Cross arm-bands did what they could for the casualties.

Settled with the South Africans, we enjoyed a week without work. At the end of it communications were reestablished with higher headquarters and we were ordered to hike seven miles to the area hardest hit. Nothing in the district had escaped the fury. A city of jagged building shells, of splintered statuary and shattered trees; every vehicle stopped, gnarled and burned, left to rust or rot in the path of the frenzied might. The only sounds other than our own were those of falling plaster and their echoes. I cannot describe the desolation properly, but I can give an idea of how it made us feel, in the words of a delirious British soldier in a makeshift P.W. hospital: "It's frightenin', I tell you. I would walk down one of them bloody streets and feel a thousand eyes on the back of me 'ead. I would 'ear 'em whisperin' behind me. I would turn around to look at 'em and there wouldn't be a bloomin' soul in sight. You can feel 'em and you can 'ear 'em but there's never anybody there." We knew what he said was so.

For "salvage" work we were divided into small crews, each under a guard. Our ghoulish mission was to search for bodies. It was rich hunting that day and the many thereafter. We started on a small scale—here a leg, there an arm, and an occasional baby—but struck a mother lode before noon. We cut our way through a basement wall to discover a reeking hash of over one hundred human beings. Flame must have swept through before the building's collapse sealed the exits, because the flesh of those within resembled the texture of prunes. Our job, it was explained, was to wade into the shambles and bring forth the remains. Encouraged by cuffing and guttural abuse, wade in we did. We did exactly that, for the floor was covered with an unsavory broth from burst water mains and viscera. A number of victims, not killed outright, had attempted to escape through a narrow emergency exit. At any rate, there were several bodies packed tightly into the passageway. Their leader had made it halfway up the steps before he was buried up to his neck in falling brick and plaster. He was about fifteen, I think.

It is with some regret that I here besmirch the nobility of our airmen, but boys, you killed an appalling lot of women and children. The shelter I have described and innumerable others like it were filled with them. We had to exhume their bodies and carry them to mass funeral pyres in the parks— so I know. The funeral pyre technique was abandoned when it became apparent how great was the toll. There was not enough labor to do it nicely, so a man with a flame-thrower was sent down instead, and he cremated them where they lay. Burned alive, suffocated, crushed—men, women, and children indiscriminately killed. For all the sublimity of the cause for which we fought, we surely created a Belsen of our own. The method was impersonal, but the result was equally cruel and heartless. That, I am afraid, is a sickening truth.

When we had become used to the darkness, the odor, and the carnage, we began musing as to what each of the corpses had been in life. It was a sordid game: "Rich man, poor man, beggar man, thief . . ." Some had fat purses and jewelry, others had precious foodstuffs. A boy had his dog still leashed to him. Renegade Ukrainians in German uniform were in charge of our operations in the shelters proper. They were roaring drunk from adjacent wine cellars and seemed to enjoy their job hugely. It was a profitable one, for they stripped each body of valuables before we carried it to the street. Death became so commonplace that we could joke about our dismal burdens and cast them about like so much garbage. Not so with the first of them, especially the young: we had lifted them onto the stretchers with care, laying them out with some semblance of funeral dignity in their last resting place before the pyre. But our awed and sorrowful propriety gave way, as I said, to rank callousness. At the end of a grisly day we would smoke and survey the impressive heap of dead accumulated. One of us flipped his cigarette butt into the pile: "Hell's bells," he said, "I'm ready for Death anytime he wants to come after me."

A few days after the raid the sirens screamed again. The listless and heartsick survivors were showered this time with leaflets. I lost my copy of the epic, but remember that it ran something like this: "To the people of Dresden: We were

forced to bomb your city because of the heavy military traffic your railroad facilities have been carrying. We realize
that we haven't always hit our objectives. Destruction of
anything other than military objectives was unintentional,
unavoidable fortunes of war." That explained the slaughter
to everyone's satisfaction, I am sure, but it aroused no little
contempt for the American bomb-sight. It is a fact that
forty-eight hours after the last B-17 had droned west for a
well-earned rest, labor battalions had swarmed over the
damaged rail yards and restored them to nearly normal
service. None of the rail bridges over the Elbe was knocked
out of commission. Bomb-sight manufacturers should
blush to know that their marvelous devices laid bombs
down as much as three miles wide of what the military
claimed to be aiming for. The leaflet should have said, "We
hit every blessed church, hospital, school, museum, theater,
your university, the zoo, and every apartment building in
town, but we honestly weren't trying hard to do it. C'est la
guerre. So sorry. Besides, saturation bombing is all the rage
these days, you know."

There was tactical significance: stop the railroads. An
excellent maneuver, no doubt, but the technique was horrible. The planes started kicking high-explosives and incendiaries through their bomb-bays at the city limits, and for
all the pattern their hits presented, they must have been
briefed by a Ouija board. Tabulate the loss against the

gain. Over one hundred thousand non-combatants and a magnificent city destroyed by bombs dropped wide of the stated objectives: the railroads were knocked out for roughly two days. The Germans counted it the greatest loss of life suffered in any single raid. The death of Dresden was a bitter tragedy, needlessly and willfully executed. The killing of children—"Jerry" children or "Jap" children, or whatever enemies the future may hold for us—can never be justified.

The facile reply to great groans such as mine is the most hateful of all clichés, "fortunes of war," and another, "They asked for it. All they understand is force." *Who* asked for it? The only thing *who* understands is force? Believe me, it is not easy to rationalize the stamping out of vineyards where the grapes of wrath are stored when gathering up babies in bushel baskets or helping a man dig where he thinks his wife may be buried. Certainly enemy military and industrial installations should have been blown flat, and woe unto those foolish enough to seek shelter near them. But the "Get Tough America" policy, the spirit of *revenge,* the approbation of all destruction and killing, has earned us a name for obscene brutality, and cost the World the possibility of Germany's becoming a peaceful and intellectually fruitful nation in anything but the most remote future.

Our leaders had a carte blanche as to what they might or

might not destroy. Their mission was to win the war as quickly as possible, and, while they were admirably trained to do just that, their decisions as to the fate of certain priceless World heirlooms—in one case Dresden—were not always judicious. When, late in the war, with the Wehrmacht breaking up on all fronts, our planes were sent to destroy this last major city, I doubt if the question was asked, "How will this tragedy benefit us, and how will that benefit compare with the ill-effects in the long run?" Dresden, a beautiful city, built in the art spirit, symbol of an admirable heritage, so anti-Nazi that Hitler visited it but twice during his whole reign, food and hospital center so bitterly needed now—plowed under and salt strewn in the furrows.

There can be no doubt that the Allies fought on the side of right and the Germans and Japanese on the side of wrong. World War II was fought for near-Holy motives. But I stand convinced that the brand of justice in which we dealt, wholesale bombings of civilian populations, was blasphemous. That the enemy did it first has nothing to do with the moral problem. What I saw of our air war, as the European conflict neared an end, had the earmarks of being an irrational war for war's sake. Soft citizens of the American democracy learned to kick a man below the belt and make the bastard scream.

The occupying Russians, when they discovered that we were Americans, embraced us and congratulated us on the complete desolation our planes had wrought. We accepted their congratulations with good grace and proper modesty, but I felt then as I feel now, that I would have given my life to save Dresden for the World's generations to come. That is how everyone should feel about every city on Earth.

THERE SHOULD
HAVE BEEN
A
SECRETARY
OF THE FUTURE.

1/10

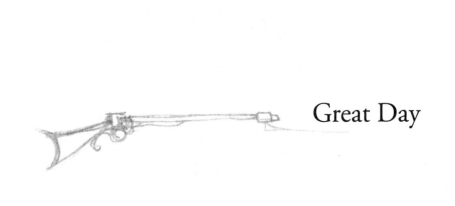

Great Day

When I was sixteen folks took me for twenty-five, and one full-growed woman from the city swore I must be thirty. I was big all over—had whiskers like steel wool. I sure wanted to see something besides LuVerne, Indiana, and that ain't saying Indianapolis would of held me, neither.

So I lied about my age, and I joined the Army of the World.

Didn't nobody cry. There wasn't no flags, there wasn't no bands. It wasn't like in olden times, where a young boy like me'd be going away to maybe get his head blowed off for democracy.

Wasn't nobody there at the depot but Ma, and Ma was mad. She thought the Army of the World was just for bums who couldn't find respectable work nowheres.

Seems like yesterday, but that was back in the year two thousand and thirty-seven.

"You keep away from them Zulus," Ma said.

"There's more'n just Zulus in the Army of the World, Ma," I told her. "There's folks from ever country there *is*."

But anybody born outside of Floyd County is a Zulu to Ma. "Well, anyways," she said, "I expect they'll feed you good, with world taxes as high as they is. And, as long as you're bound and determined to go off with them Zulus and all, I expect I ought to be glad there ain't no other armies roaming around, trying to shoot you."

"I'll be keeping the peace, Ma," I said. "Won't never be no terrible wars no more, with just one army. Don't that make you proud?"

"Makes me proud of what folks done done for peace," Ma said. "That don't make me love no army."

"It's a new, high-class kind of army, Ma," I said. "You ain't even allowed to curse. And if you don't go to church regular, you don't get no dessert."

Ma shook her head. "You just remember one thing," she said. "You just remember you *was* high-class." She didn't kiss me. She shook my hand. "As long as *I* had you," she said, "you was."

But when I sent Ma a shoulder patch from my first outfit after basic training, I heard she showed it around like it was a picture postcard from God. Wasn't nothing but a piece of blue felt with a picture of a gold clock stitched in it, and green lightning was coming out of the clock.

I heard Ma was shooting off her bazoo to everbody

about how *her* boy was in a time-screen company, just like she knowed what a time-screen company was, just like everbody knowed that was the grandest thing in the whole Army of the World.

Well, we was the first time-screen company and the last one, unless they gets the bugs out of time machines. What we was supposed to do was so secret, *we* couldn't even find out what it was till it was too late to go over the hill.

Captain Poritsky was boss, and he wouldn't tell us nothing except we should be very proud, since there was only two hundred men on the face of the earth entitled to wear them clocks.

He use to be a football player at Notre Dame, and he looked like a stack of cannonballs on a courthouse lawn. He use to like to feel hisself all over while he talked to us. He use to like to feel how hard all them cannonballs was.

He said he was real honored to be leading such a fine body of men on such a important mission. He said we'd find out what the mission was on maneuvers at a place called Château-Thierry in France.

Sometimes generals would come look at us like we was going to do something sad and beautiful, but didn't nobody say boo about no time machine.

When we got to Château-Thierry, everbody was waiting for us. That's when we found out we was supposed to be something extra-desperate. Everbody wanted to see the killers with the clocks on their sleeves, everbody wanted to see the big show we was going to put on.

If we looked wild when we got there, we got wilder as time went on. We *still* couldn't find out what a time-screen company was supposed to do.

Wasn't no use asking.

"Captain Poritsky, sir," I said to him, just as respectful as I *could* be, "I hear we are going to demonstrate some new kind of attack tomorrow at dawn."

"Smile like you was happy and proud, soldier!" he said to me. "It's true!"

"Captain, sir," I said, "our platoon done elected me to come ask you if we couldn't find out now what we is supposed to do. We want to kind of get ready, sir."

"Soldier," Poritsky said, "ever man in that platoon got morale and esprit de corps and three grenades and a rifle and a bayonet and a hundred rounds of ammunition, don't he?"

"Yes, sir," I said.

"Soldier," Poritsky said, "that platoon *is* ready. And to show you how much faith I got in that platoon, it is going to lead the attack." He raised his eyebrows. "Well," he said, "ain't you going to say, 'Thank you, sir'?"

I done it.

"And to show how much faith I got in *you*, soldier," he said, "*you* are going to be the first man in the first squad in the first platoon." His eyebrows went up again. "Ain't you going to say, 'Thank you, sir'?"

I done it again.

"Just pray the scientists is as ready as you are, soldier," Poritsky said.

"There's scientists mixed up in it, sir?" I said.

"End of interview, soldier," Poritsky said. "Come to attention, soldier."

I done it.

"Salute," Poritsky said.

I done it.

"For'd harch!" he said.

Off I went.

So there I was on the night before the big demonstration, ignorant, ascared, and homesick, on guard duty in a tunnel in France. I was on guard with a kid named Earl Sterling from Salt Lake.

"Scientists is going to help us, eh?" Earl said to me.

"That's what he said," I told him.

"I'd just as soon of *not* knowed that much," Earl said.

Up above ground a big shell went off, and liked to bust our eardrums. There was a barrage going on up above, like giants walking around, kicking the world apart. They was shells from our guns, of course, playing like they was the enemy, playing like they was sore as hell about something.

Everbody was down deep in tunnels, so wasn't nobody going to get hurt.

But wasn't nobody enjoying all that noise but Captain Poritsky, and he was crazy as a bedbug.

"Simulated this, simulated that," Earl said. "Them ain't simulated shells, and I ain't simulating being ascared of them, neither."

"Poritsky says it's music," I said.

"They say this is the way it really was, back in the real wars," Earl said. "Don't see how anybody stayed alive."

"Holes gives a lot of protection," I said.

"But back in the old days, didn't hardly nobody but generals get *down* in holes this good," Earl said. "The soldiers had shallow little things without no roof over 'em. And when the orders came, they had to get *out* of them holes, and orders like that was coming all the time."

"I expect they'd keep close to the ground," I said.

"How close can you get *to* the ground?" Earl wanted to know. "Some places up there the grass is cut down like somebody'd done used a lawn-mower. Ain't a tree left standing. Big holes everwheres. How come the folks just didn't go crazy in all them real wars—or quit?"

"Folks are funny," I said.

"Sometimes I don't think so," Earl said.

Another big shell went off, then two little ones—real quick.

"You seen that Russian company's collection?" Earl said.

"Heard about it," I said.

"They got close to a hundred skulls," Earl said. "Got 'em lined up on a shelf like honeydew melons."

"Crazy," I said.

"Yeah, collecting skulls like that," Earl said. "But they can't hardly *help* but collect 'em. I mean, they can't hardly dig in any direction and *not* find skulls and all. Something big must of happened over there."

"Something big happened all through here," I told him. "This here's a very famous battlefield from the World War. This here's where the Americans whipped the Germans. Poritsky told me."

"Two of them skulls got shrapnel in 'em," Earl said. "You seen *them*?"

"Nope," I said.

"Shake 'em, and you can hear the shrapnel rattle around inside," Earl said. "You can see the holes where the shrapnel went in."

"You know what they should ought to do with them poor skulls?" I asked him. "They should ought to get a whole slew of chaplains from ever religion there is. They should ought to give them poor skulls a decent funeral, and bury them someplace where they won't *never* be bothered again."

"It ain't like they was people any more," Earl said.

"It ain't like they wasn't *never* people," I said. "They gave up their lives so our fathers and our grandfathers and our great-grandfathers could live. The least *we* can do is treat their poor bones right."

"Yeah, but wasn't some of them trying to *kill* our great-great-grandfathers or whoever it was?" Earl said.

"The Germans *thought* they was improving things," I said. "Everbody *thought* they was improving things. Their hearts was in the right place," I said. "It's the thought that counts."

The canvas curtain at the top of the tunnel opened up, and Captain Poritsky come down from outside. He was taking his time, like there wasn't nothing out there worse'n a warm drizzle.

"Ain't it kind of dangerous, going out there, sir?" I asked him. He didn't *have* to go out there. There was tunnels running from everwheres to everwheres, and wasn't nobody supposed to go outside while the barrage was on.

"Ain't this a rather dangerous profession we picked of our own free will, soldier?" he asked me. He put the back of his hand under my nose, and I seen there was a long cut across it. "Shrapnel!" he said. He grinned, and then he stuck the cut in his mouth and sucked it.

Then, after he'd drunk enough blood to hold hisself a while, he looked me and Earl up and down. "Soldier," he said to me, "where's your bayonet?"

I felt around my belt. I'd done forgot my bayonet.

"Soldier, what if the enemy was to all of a sudden drop in?" Poritsky done a dance like he was gathering nuts in

May. "'Sorry, fellows—you wait right here while I go get my bayonet.' *That* what you'd say, soldier?" he asked me.

I shook my head.

"When the chips are down, a bayonet is a soldier's best friend," Poritsky said. "That's when a professional soldier is happiest, on account of that's when he gets to close with the enemy. Ain't that so?"

"Yes, sir," I said.

"You been collecting skulls, soldier?" Poritsky said.

"No, sir," I said.

"Wouldn't hurt you none to take it up," Poritsky said.

"No, sir," I said.

"There's a reason why ever one of 'em died, soldier," Poritsky said. "They wasn't good soldiers! They wasn't professionals! They made mistakes! They didn't learn their lessons good enough!"

"Reckon not, sir," I said.

"Maybe you think maneuvers is tough, soldier, but they ain't near tough enough," Poritsky said. "If I was in charge, everbody'd be out there taking that bombardment. Only way to get professional outfits is to get 'em blooded."

"Blooded, sir?" I said.

"Get some men killed, so's the rest can learn!" Poritsky said. "Hell—this ain't no army! They got so many safety rules and doctors, I ain't even seen a hangnail for six years. You ain't going to turn out professionals that way."

"No, sir," I said.

"The professional has seen everthing, and ain't surprised by nothing," Poritsky said. "Well, tomorrow, soldier, you're going to see real soldiering, the likes of which ain't been seen for a hundred years. Gas! Rolling barrages! Fire fights! Bayonet duels! Hand-to-hand! Ain't you glad, soldier?"

"Ain't I *what*, sir?" I said.

"Ain't you *glad*?" Poritsky said.

I looked at Earl, then back at the captain. "Oh, yes, sir," I said. I shook my head real slow and heavy. "Yes, sir," I said. "Yes, indeedy-do."

When you're in the Army of the World, with all the fancy new weapons they got, there ain't but one thing to do. You *got* to believe what the officers tell you, even if it don't make sense. And the officers, *they* got to believe what the scientists tell 'em.

Things has got that far beyond the common man, and maybe they always was. When a chaplain hollered at us enlisted men about how we got to have great faith that don't ask no questions, he was carrying coals to Newcastle.

When Poritsky finally done told us we was going to attack with the help of a time machine, there wasn't no intelligent ideas a ordinary soldier like me *could* have. I just set there like a bump on a log, and I looked at the bayonet stud on my rifle. I leaned over, so's the front of my helmet rested on the muzzle, and I looked at that there bayonet stud like it was a wonder of the world.

All two hundred of us in the time-screen company was in a big dugout, listening to Poritsky. Wasn't nobody looking at him. He was just *too* happy about what was going to happen, feeling hisself all over like he hoped he wasn't dreaming.

"Men," that crazy captain said, "at oh-five-hundred hours the artillery will lay down two lines of flares, two hundred yards apart. Them flares will mark the edges of the beam of the time machine. We will attack between them flares."

"Men," he said, "between them lines of flares it will be today and July eighteenth, nineteen-eighteen, both at the same time."

I kissed that bayonet stud. I like the taste of oil and iron in small amounts, but that ain't encouraging nobody to bottle it.

"Men," Poritsky said, "you're going to see some things out there that'd turn a civilian's hair white. You're going to see the Americans counter-attacking the Germans back in olden times at Château-Thierry." My, he *was* happy. "Men," he said, "it's going to be a slaughterhouse in Hell."

I moved my head up and down, so's my helmet acted like a pump. It pumped air down over my forehead. At a time like that, little things can be extra-nice.

"Men," Poritsky said, "I hate to tell soldiers not to be ascared. I hate to tell 'em there ain't nothing to be ascared *of.* It's an insult to 'em. But the scientists tell me nineteen-eighteen can't do nothing to us, and we can't do nothing to nineteen-eighteen. We'll be ghosts to them, and they'll be ghosts to us. We'll be walking through them and they'll be walking through us like we was all smoke."

I blowed across the muzzle of my rifle. I didn't get a tune out of it. Good thing I didn't, because it would of broke up the meeting.

"Men," Poritsky said, "I just wish you *could* take your chances back in nineteen-eighteen, take your chances with the worst they could throw at you. Them as lived through it would be soldiers in the finest sense of the word."

Nobody argued with him.

"Men," that great military scientist said, "I reckon you can imagine the effect on our enemy when he sees the battlefield crawling with all them ghosts from nineteen-eighteen. He ain't going to know *what* to shoot at." Poritsky busted out laughing, and it took him a while to pull hisself back together. "Men," he said, "we'll be creeping through them ghosts. When we reach the enemy, make him wish to God we was ghosts, too—make him sorry he was ever born."

This enemy he was talking about wasn't nothing but a line of bamboo poles with rags tied to 'em, about half a mile away. You wouldn't believe a man could hate bamboo and rags the way Poritsky done.

"Men," Poritsky said, "if anybody's thinking of going A.W.O.L., here's your golden opportunity. All you got to do is cross one of them lines of flares, go through the edge of the beam. You'll disappear into nineteen-eighteen for real—won't be nothing ghostly about it. And the M.P. ain't been born who's crazy enough to go after you, on account of can't nobody who ever crosses over come back."

I cleaned between my front teeth with my rifle sight. I figured out all by myself that a professional soldier was happiest when he could bite somebody. I knowed I wasn't never going to reach them heights.

"Men," Poritsky said, "the mission of this here time-screen company ain't no different from the mission of ever company since time began. The mission of this here time-screen company is to kill! Any questions?"

We'd all done had the Articles of War read to us. We all knowed asking sensible questions was worse'n killing your own mother with a axe. So there wasn't no questions. Don't expect there ever has been.

"Lock and load," Poritsky said.

We done it.

"Fix bayonets," Poritsky said.

We done it.

"Shall we go, girls?" Poritsky said.

Oh, that man knowed his psychology backwards and forwards. I expect that's the big difference between officers and enlisted men. Calling us girls instead of boys, when we was really boys, just made us so mad we couldn't hardly see straight.

We was going out and tear up bamboo and rags till there wasn't going to be no more fishpoles or crazy quilts for centuries.

Being in the beam of that there time machine was a cross between flu, wearing bifocals that was made for somebody else who couldn't see good, and being inside a guitar. Until they improves it, it ain't never going to be safe or popular.

We didn't see no folks from nineteen-eighteen at first. All we seen was their holes and barbed-wire, where there wasn't no holes and barbed-wire no more. We could walk over them holes like they had glass roofs over 'em. We could walk through that barbed-wire without getting our pants tore. They wasn't ours—they was nineteen-eighteen's.

There was thousands of soldiers watching us, folks from ever country there was.

The show we put on for 'em was just pitiful.

That time-machine beam made us sick to our stomachs and half blind. We was supposed to whoop it up and holler to show how professional we was. But we got out there between them flares, and didn't hardly nobody let out a peep for fear they'd throw up. We was supposed to advance aggressively, only we couldn't tell what belonged to us, and what was nineteen-eighteen's. We'd walk around things that wasn't there, and fall over things that was there.

If I had of been a observer, I would of said we was comical.

I was the first man in the first squad of the first platoon of that time-screen company, and wasn't but one man in front of me. He was our noble captain.

He only hollered one thing at his fearless troops, and I thought he hollered that to make us even more bloodthirsty than we was. "So long, Boy Scouts!" he hollered. "Write your mothers regular, and wipe your noses when they runs!"

Then he bent over, and he run off across no man's land as fast as he could go.

I done my best to stick with him, for the honor of the enlisted men. We was both falling down and getting up like a couple of drunks, just beating ourselves to pieces on that battlefield.

He never looked around to see how me and the rest was doing. I thought he didn't want nobody to see how green he was. I kept trying to tell him we'd done left everbody way behind, but the race took ever bit of breath I had.

When he headed off to one side, towards a line of flares, I figured he wanted to get in the smoke where folks couldn't see him, so he could get sick in private.

I had just fell into the smoke after him when a barrage from nineteen-eighteen hit.

That poor old world, she rocked and rolled, she spit and tore, she boiled and burned. Dirt and steel from nineteen-eighteen flew through Poritsky and me ever *which* way.

"Get up!" Poritsky hollered at me. "That's nineteen-eighteen! Can't hurt you none!"

"It would if it could!" I hollered back at him.

He made like he was going to kick me in the head. "Get up, soldier!" he said.

I done it.

"Get back with the rest of them Boy Scouts," he said. He pointed through a hole in the smoke, pointed back to where we'd come from. I seen the rest of the company was showing them thousands of observers how experts laid down and quivered. "That's where *you* belong," Poritsky said. "This here's my show, and it's a solo."

"Beg pardon?" I said. I turned my head to follow a nineteen-eighteen boulder that had just flew through *both* our heads.

"Look at me!" he hollered.

I done it.

"Here's where we separates the men from the boys, soldier," he said.

"Yes, sir," I said. "Can't hardly nobody run as fast as you can."

"I ain't talking about running," he said. "I'm talking about fighting!" Oh, it was a crazy conversation. Nineteen-eighteen tracers had started going through us.

I thought he was talking about fighting bamboo and rags. "Ain't nobody feeling very good, Captain, but I expect we'll win," I said.

"I mean I'm going through these here flares to nineteen-eighteen!" he hollered. "Ain't nobody else man enough to do that. Now, get the hell out of here!"

I seen he wasn't fooling a bit. He really did think that'd be grand, if he could wave a flag and stop a bullet, even if it was in some war that'd been over for a hundred years or more. He wanted to get in his lick, even if the ink on the peace treaties was so faded you couldn't hardly read them no more.

"Captain," I said to him, "I ain't nothing but a enlisted man, and enlisted men ain't even supposed to hint. But Captain," I said, "I don't think that makes good sense."

"I was born to *fight*!" he hollered. "I'm rusting out inside!"

"Captain," I said, "everthing there *is* to fight for has already done been won. We got peace, we got freedom, everbody everwhere is like brothers, everbody got nice houses and chicken ever Sunday."

He didn't hear me. He was walking towards the line of flares, towards the edge of the time-machine beam, where the smoke from the flares was thickest.

He stopped just before he got into nineteen-eighteen forever. He looked down at something, and I thought maybe he'd done found a bird's nest or a daisy in no man's land.

What he'd found wasn't neither. I went up to him and seen he was standing over a nineteen-eighteen shell hole, just like he was hanging in air.

There was two dead men in that sorry hole, two live ones, and mud. I knowed that two was dead, on account of one didn't have no head, and the other was blowed in two.

If you got a heart, and you come on something like that in a thick smoke, ain't nothing else in this universe going to be real. There wasn't no more Army of the World; there wasn't no more peace everlasting; there wasn't no more LuVerne, Indiana; there wasn't no more time machine.

There was just Poritsky and me and the hole.

If I was ever to have a child, this is what I'd tell it: "Child," I'd say, "don't never mess with time. Keep now now and then then. And if you ever get lost in thick smoke, child, set still till it clears. Set still till you can see where you are and where you been and where you're going, child."

I'd shake that child. "Child, you hear?" I'd say. "You listen to what your Daddy says. He *know*."

Ain't never going to see no sweet child of mine, I expect. But I aims to feel one, smell one, and hear one. Damn if I don't.

You could see where the four poor nineteen-eighteen souls had been crawling around and around in that hole, like snails crawling around in a fishbowl. There was a track leading from each one—the live ones *and* the dead ones.

A shell lit in the hole and blowed up.

When the mud fell back down, there wasn't but one man left alive.

He turned over from his belly to his back, and he let his arms flop out. It was like he was offering his soft parts to nineteen-eighteen, so it could kill him easy, if it wanted to kill him so bad.

And then *he* seen *us*.

He wasn't surprised to see us hanging there in air over him. Wasn't nothing could surprise *him* no more. Real slow and clumsy, he dug his rifle out of the mud and aimed it at us. He smiled like he knowed who we was, like he knowed he couldn't hurt us none, like it was all a big joke.

There wasn't no way a bullet could get through that rifle bore, it was so clogged with mud. The rifle blowed up.

That didn't surprise him none, neither, didn't even seem to hurt. That smile he give us, the smile about the joke, was still there when he laid back and died.

The nineteen-eighteen barrage stopped.

Somebody blowed a whistle from way far off.

"What you crying about, soldier?" Poritsky said.

"I didn't know I was, Captain," I said. My skin felt extra-tight, and my eyes was hot, but I didn't know I was crying.

"You was and you are," he said.

Then I really *did* cry. I knowed for sure I was just sixteen, knowed I wasn't nothing but a over-growed baby. I set down, and I swore I wouldn't get up again, even if the captain kicked my head off.

"There they go!" Poritsky hollered, real wild. "Look, soldier, look! Americans!" He fired his pistol off like it was the Fourth of July. "Look!"

I done it.

Looked like a million men crossing the beam of the time machine. They'd come from nothing on one side, melt away to nothing on the other. Their eyes was dead. They put one foot in front of the other like somebody'd wound 'em up.

All of a sudden, Captain Poritsky hauled me up like I didn't weigh nothing. "Come on, soldier—we're going with 'em!" he hollered.

That crazy man drug me right through that line of flares. I screamed and I cried and I bit him. But it was too late. There wasn't no flares no more.

There wasn't nothing but nineteen-eighteen all around.

I was in nineteen-eighteen for good.

And then another barrage hit. And it was steel and high-explosive, and I was flesh, and then was then, and steel and flesh was all balled up together.

I woke up here.

"What year is it?" I asked 'em.

"Nineteen-eighteen, soldier," they said.

"Where am I?" I asked 'em.

They told me I was in a cathedral that'd been turned into

a hospital. Wish I could see it. I can hear from the echoes how high and grand it is.

I ain't no hero.

With heroes all around me here, I don't embroider my record none. I never bayoneted or shot nobody, never throwed a grenade, never even seen a German, unless them was Germans in that terrible hole.

They should ought to have special hospitals for heroes, so heroes wouldn't have to lay next to the likes of me.

When somebody new comes around to hear me talk, I always tell 'em right off I wasn't in the war but ten seconds before I was hit. "I never done a thing to make the world safe for democracy," I tell 'em. "When I got hit, I was crying like a baby and trying to kill my own captain. If a bullet hadn't of killed him, *I would* of, and he was a fellow American."

I would of, too.

And I tell 'em I'd desert back to the year two thousand and thirty-seven, too, if I got half a chance.

There's two court-martial offenses right there.

But all these heroes here, they don't seem to care. "That's all right, Buddy," they say, "you just go right on talking. If somebody tries to court-martial you, we'll all swear we seen you killing Germans with your bare hands, and fire coming out of your ears."

They likes to hear me talk.

So I lay here, blind as a bat, and I tell 'em how I got here. I tell 'em all the things I see so clear inside my head—the Army of the World, everbody like brothers everwhere, peace everlasting, nobody hungry, nobody ascared.

That's how come I got my nickname. Don't hardly nobody in the hospital know my real name. Don't know who thought of it first, but everbody calls me Great Day.

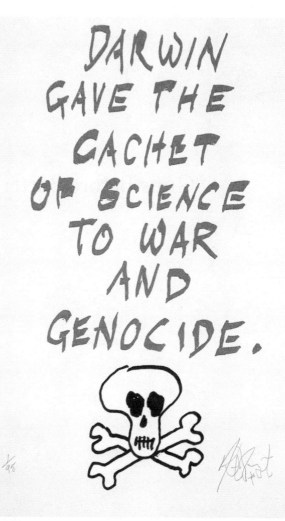

Guns Before Butter

I.

What you do is take a roasting chicken, cut it up into pieces, and brown it in melted butter and olive oil in a hot skillet," said Private Donnini. "A good, hot skillet," he added thoughtfully.

"Wait a minute," said Private Coleman, writing furiously in a small notebook. "How big a chicken?"

"About four pounds."

"For how many people?" asked Private Kniptash sharply.

"Enough for four," said Donnini.

"Don't forget, a lot of that chicken is bone," said Kniptash suspiciously.

Donnini was a gourmet; many was the time that the phrase "pearls before swine" had occurred to him while telling Kniptash how to make this dish or that. Kniptash cared nothing for flavor or aroma—cared only for brute nutrition, for caloric blockbusters. In taking down recipes in his notebook, Kniptash was inclined to regard the portions as niggardly, and to double all the quantities involved.

"You can eat it all yourself, as far as I'm concerned," said Donnini evenly.

"O.K., O.K., so what do you do next?" said Coleman, his pencil poised.

"You brown it on each side for about five minutes, add chopped celery, onions, and carrots, and season to taste." Donnini pursed his lips as though sampling. "Then, while you're simmering it, add a mixture of sherry and tomato paste. Cover it. Simmer for around thirty minutes, and—" He paused. Coleman and Kniptash had stopped writing, and were leaning against the wall, their eyes closed—listening.

"That's good," said Kniptash dreamily, "but you know the first thing I'm gonna get back in the States?"

Donnini groaned inwardly. He knew. He had heard it a hundred times. Kniptash was sure there wasn't a dish in the world that could satisfy his hunger, so he had invented one, a culinary monster.

"First," said Kniptash fiercely, "I'm going to order me a dozen pancakes. That's what I said, Lady," he said, addressing an imaginary waitress, "twelve! Then I'm going to have 'em stack 'em up with a fried egg between each one. Then you know what I'm going to do?"

"Pour honey over 'em!" said Coleman. He shared Kniptash's brutish appetite.

"You betcha!" said Kniptash, his eyes glistening.

"Phooey," said Corporal Kleinhans, their bald German

guard, listlessly. Donnini guessed that the old man was about sixty-five years old. Kleinhans tended to be absent-minded, lost in thought. He was an oasis of compassion and inefficiency in the desert of Nazi Germany. He said he had learned his passable English during four years as a waiter in Liverpool. He would say no more about his experiences in England, other than to observe that the British ate far more food than was good for the race.

Kleinhans twisted his Kaiser Wilhelm mustache, and stood with the help of his antique, six-foot-long rifle. "You talk too much about food. That is why the Americans will lose the war—you are all too soft." He looked pointedly at Kniptash, who was still up to his nostrils in imaginary cakes, eggs, and honey. "Come, come, back to work." It was a suggestion.

The three American soldiers remained seated within the roofless shell of a building amid the smashed masonry and timbers of Dresden, Germany. The time was early March, 1945. Kniptash, Donnini, and Coleman were prisoners of war. Corporal Kleinhans was their guard. He was to keep them busy at arranging the city's billion tons of rubble into orderly cairns, rock by rock, out of the way of non-existent traffic. Nominally, the three Americans were being punished for minor defections in prison discipline. Actually, their being marched out to work in the streets every morning under the sad blue eyes of the lackadaisical Kleinhans was no better, no worse than the fates of their better-behaved comrades behind the barbed-wire. Kleinhans asked only that they appear to be busy when officers passed.

Food was the only thing on the P.W.'s pale level of existence that could have any effect on their spirits. Patton was a hundred miles away. To hear Kniptash, Donnini, and Coleman speak of the approaching Third Army, one would have thought it was spear-headed, not by infantry and tanks, but by a phalanx of mess sergeants and kitchen trucks.

"Come, come," said Corporal Kleinhans again. He brushed plaster dust from his ill-fitting uniform, the thin, cheap grey of the homeguard, the pathetic army of old men. He looked at his watch. Their lunch hour, which had been thirty minutes with nothing to eat, was over.

Donnini wistfully leafed through his notebook for another minute before returning it to his breast pocket and struggling to his feet.

The notebook craze had begun with Donnini's telling Coleman how to make Pizza pie. Coleman had written it down in one of several notebooks he had taken from a bombed-out stationery store. He had found the experience so satisfying, that all three were soon obsessed with filling the notebooks with recipes. Setting down the symbols for food somehow made them feel much closer to the real thing.

Each had divided his booklet into departments. Kniptash, for instance, had four major departments: "Desserts

I Am Going to Try," "Good Ways to Fix Meat," "Snacks,"
and "Missalanious."

Coleman, scowling, continued to print laboriously in his
notebook. "How much sherry?"

"Dry sherry—it's got to be *dry*," said Donnini. "About
three-quarters of a cup." He saw that Kniptash was erasing
something in his notebook. "What's the matter? Changing
it to a gallon of sherry?"

"Nope. Wasn't even working on that one. I was changing
something else. Changed my mind about what the first
thing I want is," said Kniptash.

"What?" asked Coleman, fascinated.

Donnini winced. So did Kleinhans. The notebooks had
heightened the spiritual conflict between Donnini and
Kniptash, had defined it in black and white. The recipes
that Kniptash contributed were flamboyant, made up on
the spot. Donnini's were scrupulously authentic, artistic.
Coleman was caught between. It was gourmet versus glut-
ton, artist versus materialist, beauty versus the beast. Donnini was grateful for an ally, even Corporal Kleinhans.

"Don't tell me yet," said Coleman, flipping pages.
"Wait'll I get set with the first page." The most important
section of each of the notebooks was, by far, the first page.
By agreement, it was dedicated to the dish each man looked
forward to above all others. On his first page, Donnini
had lovingly inscribed the formula for *Anitra al Cognac*—
brandied duck. Kniptash had given the place of honor to

his pancake horror. Coleman had plumped uncertainly for ham and candied sweet potatoes, but had been argued out of it. Terribly torn, he had written both Kniptash's and Donnini's selections on his first page, putting off a decision until a later date. Now, Kniptash was tantalizing him with a modification of his atrocity. Donnini sighed. Coleman was weak. Perhaps Kniptash's new twist would woo him away from *Anitra al Cognac* altogether.

"Honey's out," said Kniptash firmly. "I kind of wondered about it. Now I know it's all wrong. Doesn't go with eggs, honey doesn't."

Coleman erased. "Well?" he said expectantly.

"Hot fudge on top," said Kniptash. "A big blob of hot fudge—just let 'er set on top and spread out."

"Mmmmmmmmmmmm," said Coleman.

"Food, food, food," muttered Corporal Kleinhans. "All day, every day, all I hear is food! Get up. Get to work! You and your damn fool notebooks. That's plundering, you know. I can shoot you for that." He closed his eyes and sighed. "Food," he said softly. "What good does it do to talk about it, to write about it? Talk about girls. Talk about music. Talk about liquor." He implored Heaven with outstretched arms. "What kind of soldiers are these that spend all day exchanging recipes?"

"You're hungry, too, aren't you?" said Kniptash. "What have you got against food?"

"I get quite enough to eat," said Kleinhans off-handedly.

"Six slices of black bread and three bowls of soup a day—that's enough?" said Coleman.

"That's plenty," argued Kleinhans. "I feel better. I was overweight before the war. Now I'm as trim as I was as a young man. Before the war, everybody was overweight, living to eat instead of eating to live." He smiled wanly. "Germany has never been healthier."

"Yeah, but aren't you hungry?" persisted Kniptash.

"Food isn't the only thing in my life, nor the most important." said Kleinhans. "Come, now, get up!"

Kniptash and Coleman arose reluctantly. "Got plaster or something in the end of your barrel, Pop," said Coleman. They shuffled slowly back onto the littered street, with Kleinhans bringing up the rear, digging plaster from his rifle muzzle with a match, and denouncing the notebooks.

Donnini picked out a small rock from millions, carried it over to the curb and lay it at the feet of Kleinhans. He rested for a moment, his hands on his hips. "Hot," he said.

"Just right for working," said Kleinhans. He sat down on the curb. "What were you in civilian life, a cook?" he said after a long silence.

"I helped my father run his Italian restaurant in New York."

"I had a place in Breslau for a while," said Kleinhans. "That was long ago." He sighed. "Seems silly now how much time and energy Germans used to spend just stuffing themselves with rich food. Such a silly waste." He looked past Donnini and glared. He waggled a finger at Coleman and Kniptash, who stood together in the middle of the street, each with a baseball-sized rock in one hand, a notebook in the other.

"It seems to me there was sour cream in it," Coleman was saying.

"Put those books away!" commanded Kleinhans. "Haven't you got a girl? Talk about your girl!"

"Sure I got a girl," said Coleman irritably. "Name's Mary."

"Is that *all* there is to know about her?" said Kleinhans.

Coleman looked puzzled. "Last name's Fiske—Mary Fiske."

"Well, is this Mary Fiske pretty? What does she do?"

Coleman narrowed his eyes thoughtfully. "One time I was waiting for her to come downstairs and I watched her old lady make a lemon meringue pie," he said. "What she did was take some sugar and some cornstarch and a pinch of salt, and mix it in with a couple of cups of wat—"

"Please, let's talk about music. Like music?" said Kleinhans.

"And then what'd she do?" said Kniptash. He had•laid his rock down, and was now writing in his notebook. "She used eggs, didn't she?"

"Please, boys, no," pleaded Kleinhans.

"Sure she used eggs," said Coleman. "And butter, too. Plenty of butter and eggs."

II.

It was four days later that Kniptash found the crayons in a basement—on the same day that Kleinhans had begged for and been refused relief from the punishment detail.

When they had set out that morning, Kleinhans had been in a terrible temper, and had railed at his three charges for not keeping in step and for marching with their hands in their pockets. "Go ahead and talk, talk, talk about food, you women," he had taunted them. "I don't have to listen anymore!" Triumphantly, he had pulled two wads of cotton from his cartridge pouch and stuffed them into his ears. "Now I can think my own thoughts. Ha!"

At noon, Kniptash sneaked into the cellar of a bombed-out house, hoping for a rack of full mason jars such as he knew were in his snug cellar at home. He emerged dirty and dispirited, gnawing experimentally at a green crayon.

"How is it?" asked Coleman hopefully, looking at the yellow, purple, pink, and orange crayons in Kniptash's left hand.

"Wonderful. What flavor you like? Lemon? Grape? Strawberry?" He threw the crayons on the ground, and spit the green one after them.

It was lunch hour again, and Kleinhans was sitting with his back to his wards, staring thoughtfully out at the splintered Dresden skyline. Two white tufts protruded from his ears.

"You know what would go good, now?" said Donnini.

"A hot fudge sundae, with nuts and marshmallow topping," said Coleman promptly.

"And cherries," said Kniptash.

"Spiedini alla Romana!" whispered Donnini, his eyes closed.

Kniptash and Coleman whipped out their notebooks.

Donnini kissed his fingertips. "Skewered chopped beef, Roman style," he said. "Take a pound of chopped beef, two eggs, three tablespoons of Romano cheese, and—"

"For how many?" demanded Kniptash.

"Six normal human beings, or half a pig."

"What's this stuff look like?" asked Coleman.

"Well, it's a lot of stuff strung together on a skewer." Donnini saw Kleinhans remove an ear plug and return it almost instantly. "It's kind of hard to describe." He scratched his head, and his gaze landed on the crayons. He picked up the yellow one, and began to sketch. He became interested in the project, and, with the other crayons, added the subtler shadings and highlights, and finally, for background, a checkered tablecloth. He handed it to Coleman.

"Mmmmmmmm," said Coleman, shaking his head and licking his lips.

"Boy!" said Kniptash admiringly. "The little bastards practically jump out at you, don't they!"

Coleman held out his notebook eagerly. The page it was

opened to was headed, straightforwardly, "CAKES." "Could you draw a Lady Baltimore cake? You know, white with cherries on top?"

Obligingly, Donnini tried, and met with heartening success. It was a fine-looking cake, and, for an added flourish, he sketched in pink icing script on top: "Welcome home Private Coleman!"

"Draw me a stack of pancakes—twelve of 'em," urged Kniptash. "That's what I said, Lady—twelve!" Donnini shook his head disapprovingly, but began to rough in the composition.

"I'm going to show *mine* to Kleinhans," said Coleman happily, holding his Lady Baltimore cake at arm's length.

"Now the fudge on top," said Kniptash, breathing down Donnini's neck.

"Ach! Mensch!" cried Corporal Kleinhans, and Coleman's notebook fluttered like a wounded bird into the tangle of wreckage next door. "The lunch hour is over!" He strode over to Donnini and Kniptash, and snatched their notebooks from them. He stuffed the books into his breast pocket. "Now we draw pretty pictures! Back to work, do you understand?" With a flourish, he fastened a fantastically long bayonet on to his rifle. "Go! *Los!*"

"What the hell got into him?" said Kniptash.

"All I did was show him a picture of a cake and he blows his stack," complained Coleman. "Nazi," he said under his breath.

Donnini slipped the crayons into his pocket, and scrambled out of the way of Kleinhans' terrible swift sword.

"The Articles of the Geneva Convention say privates must work for their keep. Work!" said Corporal Kleinhans. He kept them sweating and grunting all afternoon. He barked an order the instant any of the three showed an inclination to speak. "You! Donnini! Here, pick up this bowl of spaghetti," he said, indicating a huge boulder with the tip of his toe. He strode over to a pair of twelve-by-twelve rafters lying across the street. "Kniptash and Coleman, my boys," he crooned, clapping his hands, "here are those chocolate éclairs you've been dreaming about. One for each of you." He placed his face an inch from Coleman's. "With whipped cream," he whispered.

It was a genuinely glum crew that shambled into the prison enclosure that evening. Before, Donnini, Kniptash, and Coleman had made a point of half limping in, as though beaten down by terribly hard labor and unrelenting discipline. Kleinhans, in turn, had made a fine spectacle, snapping at them like a bad-tempered sheep dog as they stumbled through the gate. Now, their semblance was as before, but the tragedy they portrayed was real.

Kleinhans jerked open the barracks door, and motioned them in with an imperious sweep of his hand.

"Achtung!" cried a high voice from within. Donnini, Coleman, and Kniptash halted and slouched, their heels more or less together. With a crackle of leather and the

clack of heels, Corporal Kleinhans slammed his rifle butt on the floor, and stood as erect as his old back would permit, trembling. A surprise inspection by a German officer was under way. Once a month they could expect one. A short colonel in a fur-collared coat and black boots was standing, his feet far apart, before a rank of prisoners. Beside him was the fat sergeant of the guard. All stared at Corporal Kleinhans and his charges.

"Well," said the colonel in German, "what have we here?"

The sergeant hurriedly explained with gestures, his brown eyes pleading for approval.

The colonel walked slowly across the cement floor, his hands clasped behind his back. He paused before Kniptash. "You pin a pad poy, eh?"

"Yessir, I have," said Kniptash simply.

"You sorry now?"

"Yessir, I sure am."

"Good." The colonel circled the small group several times, humming to himself, pausing once to finger the fabric of Donnini's shirt. "You unnerstandt me ven I talk Enklish?"

"Yessir, it's very clear," said Donnini.

"Vot part von Amerika I got an agsent like?" he asked eagerly.

"Milwaukee, sir. I could have sworn you were from Milwaukee."

"I could be a spvy in Milvaukee," said the colonel

proudly to the sergeant. Suddenly, his gaze fell on Corporal Kleinhans, whose chest was just a little below his eye-level. His good humor evaporated. He stalked over to stand squarely before Kleinhans. "Corporal! Your blouse pocket is unbuttoned!" he said in German.

Kleinhans' eyes were wide as he reached for the offending pocket flap. Feverishly, he tried to tug it down to the button. It wouldn't reach.

"You have something in your pocket!" said the colonel, reddening. "*That's* the trouble. Take it out!"

Kleinhans jerked two notebooks from the pocket and buttoned the flap. He sighed with relief.

"And what have you in your notebooks, eh? A list of prisoners. Demerits, maybe? Let me see them." The colonel snatched them from the limp fingers. Kleinhans rolled his eyes.

"What is this?" said the colonel incredulously, his voice high. Kleinhans started to speak. "Silence, Corporal!" The colonel raised his eyebrows, and held a book out so that the sergeant could share his view. "'Vot I am going to eat de first ting ven I gat home,'" he read slowly. He shook his head. "Ach! 'Tvelf pangakes mit a fried ek betveen each von!' Oh! 'Und mit hot futch on top!'" He turned to Kleinhans. "Is that what you want, you poor boy?" he said in German. "And such a pretty picture you drew, too. Mmmmm." He reached for Kleinhans' shoulders. "Corporals have to think about war all the time. Privates can think about anything they want to—girls, food, and good things like that—just as long as they do what the corporals tell them." Deftly, as though he'd done it many times before, the colonel dug his thumbnails beneath the silver corporal's pips on Kleinhans' shoulder loops. They rattled against the wall like pebbles, down at the far end of the barracks. "Lucky privates."

Once more, Kleinhans cleared his throat for permission to speak.

"Silence, Private!" The little colonel strutted out of the barracks, shredding the notebooks as he went.

III.

Donnini felt rotten, and so, he knew, did Kniptash and Coleman. It was the morning after Kleinhans' demotion. Outwardly, Kleinhans seemed no different. His stride was spry as ever, and he still seemed capable of drawing pleasure from the fresh air and signs of spring poking up from the ruins.

When they arrived at their street, which still wasn't passable, even to bicycles, despite their three weeks of punishment, Kleinhans didn't browbeat them as he had the afternoon before. Neither did he tell them to appear to be busy as he had done the days before that. Instead, he led them directly into the ruin where they spent their lunch hours, and motioned them to sit down. Kleinhans appeared to sleep. There they sat in silence, the Americans aching with remorse.

"We're sorry you lost your pips on account of us," said Donnini at last.

"Lucky privates," said Kleinhans gloomily. "Two wars I go through to be a corporal. Now," he snapped his fingers, "poof. Cookbooks are *verboten*."

"Here," said Kniptash, his voice quavering. "Want a smoke? I got a Hungarian cigarette." He held out the precious cigarette.

Kleinhans smiled wanly. "Let's pass it around." He lit it, took a puff, and handed it to Donnini.

"Where'd you get a Hungarian cigarette?" asked Coleman.

"From a Hungarian," said Kniptash. He pulled up his trouser legs. "Traded my socks for it."

They finished the cigarette and leaned back against the masonry. Still Kleinhans had said nothing about work. Again he seemed faraway, lost in thought.

"Don't you boys talk about food anymore?" said Kleinhans, after another long silence.

"Not after you lost your pips," said Kniptash gravely.

Kleinhans nodded. "That's all right. Easy come, easy go." He licked his lips. "Pretty soon now, this will all be over." He leaned back and stretched. "And you know what I'm going to do the day it ends, boys?" Private Kleinhans closed his eyes. "I'm going to get three pounds of beef shoulder and lard it with bacon. Then I'll rub it with garlic and salt and pepper, and put it in a crock with white wine and water"—his voice became strident—"and onions and bay leaves and sugar"—he stood—"and peppercorns! In ten days, boys, she's ready!"

"What's ready?" said Coleman excitedly, reaching where his notebook had been.

"Sauerbraten!" cried Kleinhans.

"For how many?" asked Kniptash.

"Just two, my boy. Sorry." Kleinhans laid his hand on Donnini's shoulder. "Enough sauerbraten for two hungry artists—eh, Donnini?" He winked at Kniptash. "For you and Coleman, I'll fix something very filling. How about twelve pancakes with a slice of colonel between each one, and a big blob of hot fudge on top, eh?"

DO NOT BE ALARMED.
THE MAN WHO GAVE
YOU THIS NOTE IS AN
AIR RAID WARDEN.
LIE DOWN ON YOUR
BACK AND DO WHAT
HE SAYS.

Happy Birthday, 1951

S ummer is a fine time for a birthday," said the old man. "And, as long as you have a choice, why not choose a summer day?" He wet his thumb on his tongue, and leafed through the sheaf of documents the soldiers had ordered him to fill out. No document could be complete without a birthdate, and, for the boy, one had to be chosen.

"Today can be your birthday, if you like it," said the old man.

"It rained in the morning," said the boy.

"All right, then—tomorrow. The clouds are blowing off to the south. The sun should shine all day tomorrow."

Looking for shelter from the morning rainstorm, the soldiers had found the hidingplace where, miracle of miracles, the old man and the boy had lived in the ruins for seven years without documents—without, as it were, official permission to be alive. They said no person could get food or shelter or clothing without documents. But the old man and the boy had found all three for the digging in the catacombs of cellars beneath the shattered city, for the filching at night.

"Why are you shaking?" said the boy.

"Because I'm old. Because soldiers frighten old men."

"They don't frighten me," said the boy. He was excited by the sudden intrusion into their underground world. He held something shiny, golden in the narrow shaft of light from the cellar window. "See? One of them gave me a brass button."

There had been nothing frightening about the soldiers. Since the man was so old and the child so young, the military took a playful view of the pair—who, of all the people in the city, alone had recorded their presence nowhere, had been inoculated against nothing, had sworn allegiance to nothing, renounced or apologized for nothing, voted or marched for nothing, since the war.

"I meant no harm," the old man had told the soldiers with a pretence of senility. "I didn't know." He told them how, on the day the war ended, a refugee woman had left a baby in his arms and never returned. That was how he got the boy. The child's nationality? Name? Birthdate? He didn't know.

The old man rolled potatoes from the stove's wood fire with a stick, knocked the embers from their blackened skins. "I haven't been a very good father, letting you go without birthdays this long," he said. "You're entitled to one every year, you know, and I've let six years go by without a birthday. And presents, too. You're supposed to get presents." He picked up a potato gingerly, and tossed it to the boy, who caught it and laughed. "So you've decided tomorrow's the day, eh?"

"Yes, I think so."

"All right. That doesn't give me much time to get you a present, but there'll be something."

"What?"

"Birthday presents are better if they're a surprise." He thought of the wheels he had seen on a pile of rubble down the street. When the boy fell asleep, he would make some sort of cart.

"Listen!" said the boy.

As at every sunset, over the ruins from a distant street came the sound of marching.

"Don't listen," said the old man. He held up a finger for attention. "And you know what we'll do on your birthday?"

"Steal cakes from the bakery?"

"Maybe—but that isn't what I was thinking of. You know what I'd like to do tomorrow? I'd like to take you where you've never been in all your life—where I haven't been for years." The thought made the old man excited and happy. This would be *the* gift. The cart would be nothing. "Tomorrow I'll take you away from war."

He didn't see that the boy looked puzzled, and a little disappointed.

. . .

It was the birthday the boy had chosen for himself, and the sky, as the old man had promised, was clear. They ate breakfast in the twilight of their cellar. The cart the old man had made late at night sat on the table. The boy ate with one hand, his other hand resting on the cart. Occasionally, he paused in eating to move the cart back and forth a few inches, and to imitate the sound of a motor.

"That's a nice truck you've got there, Mister," said the old man. "Bringing animals to the market, are you?"

"Brummmaaaa, brummmaaaa. Out of my way! Brummmaaaa. Out of the way of my tank."

"Sorry," sighed the old man, "thought you were a truck. You like it anyway, and that's what counts." He dropped his tin plate into the bucket of water simmering on the stove. "And this is only the beginning, only the beginning," he said expansively. "The best is yet to come."

"Another present?"

"In a way. Remember what I promised? We'll get away from war today. We'll go to the woods."

"Brummmaaaa, brummmaaaa. Can I take my tank?"

"If you'll let it be a truck, just for today."

The boy shrugged. "I'll leave it, and play with it when I get back."

Blinking in the bright morning, the two walked down their deserted street, turned into a busy boulevard lined with brave new façades. It was as though the world had suddenly become fresh and clean and whole again. The people didn't seem to know that desolation began a block on either side of the fine boulevard, and stretched for miles. The two, with lunches under their arms, walked toward the pine-covered hills to the south, toward which the boulevard lifted in a gentle grade.

Four young soldiers came down the sidewalk abreast. The old man stepped into the street, out of their way. The boy saluted, and held his ground. The soldiers smiled, returned his salute, and parted their ranks to let him pass.

"Armored infantry," said the boy to the old man.

"Hmmmm?" said the old man absently, his eyes on the green hills. "Really? How did you know that?"

"Didn't you see the green braid?"

"Yes, but those things change. I can remember when armored infantry was black and red, and green was—" He cut the sentence short. "It's all nonsense," he said, almost sharply. "It's all meaningless, and today we're going to forget all about it. Of all days, on your birthday, you shouldn't be thinking about—"

"Black and red is the engineers," interrupted the boy seriously. "Plain black is the military police, and red is the artillery, and blue and red is the medical corps, and black and orange is . . ."

The pine forest was very still. The centuries-old carpet of needles and green roof deadened the sounds floating up from the city. Infinite colonnades of thick brown trunks surrounded the old man and the boy. The sun, directly overhead, showed itself to them only as a cluster of bright pinpoints through the fat, dense blanket of needles and boughs above.

"Here?" said the boy.

The old man looked about himself. "No—just a little farther." He pointed. "There—see through there? We can see the church from here." The black skeleton of a burned steeple was framed against a square of sky between two trunks on the edge of the forest. "But listen—hear that? Water. There's a brook up above, and we can get down in its little valley and see nothing but treetops and sky."

"All right," said the boy. "I like this place, but all right." He looked at the steeple, then at the old man, and raised his eyebrows questioningly.

"You'll see—you'll see how much better," said the old man.

As they reached the top of the ridge, he gestured happily at the brook below. "There! And what do you think of this? Eden! As it was in the beginning—trees, sky, and water. This is the world you should have had, and today, at least, you can have it."

"And look!" said the boy, pointing to the ridge on the other side.

A huge tank, rusted to the color of the fallen pine needles, squatted on shattered treads on the ridge, with scabs of corrosion about the black hole where its gun had once been.

"How can we cross the water to get to it?" said the boy.

"We don't want to get to it," said the old man irritably. He held the boy's hand tightly. "Not today. Some other day we can come out here, maybe. But not today."

The boy was crestfallen. His small hand grew limp in the old man's.

"Here's a bend up ahead, and around that we'll find exactly what we want."

The boy said nothing. He snatched up a rock, and threw it at the tank. As the little missile fell toward the target, he tensed, as though the whole world were about to explode. A faint click came from the turret, and he relaxed, somehow satisfied. Docilely, he followed the old man.

Around the bend, they found what the old man had been looking for: a smooth, dry table of rock, out by the stream, walled in by high banks. The old man stretched out on the moss, affectionately patted the spot beside him, where he wanted the boy to sit. He unwrapped his lunch.

After lunch, the boy fidgeted. "It's very quiet," he said at last.

"It's as it should be," said the old man. "One corner of the world—as it should be."

"It's lonely."

"That's its beauty."

"I like it better in the city, with the soldiers and—"

The old man seized his arm roughly, squeezed it hard. "No you don't. You just don't know. You're too young, too young to know what this is, what I'm trying to give you. But, when you're older, you'll remember, and want to come back here—long after your little cart is broken."

"I don't want my cart to be broken," said the boy.

"It won't, it won't. But just lie here, close your eyes and listen, and forget about everything. This much I can give you—a few hours away from war." He closed his eyes.

The boy lay down beside him, and dutifully closed his eyes, too.

The sun was low in the sky when the old man awakened. He ached and felt damp from his long nap by the brook. He yawned and stretched. "Time to go," he said, his eyes still closed. "Our day of peace is over." And then he saw that the boy was gone. He called the boy's name unconcernedly at first; and then, getting no answer but the wind's, he stood and shouted.

Panic welled up in him. The boy had never been in the woods before, could easily get lost if he were to wander north, deeper into the hills and forest. He climbed onto higher ground and shouted again. No answer.

Perhaps the boy had gone down to the tank again, and tried to cross the stream. He couldn't swim. The old man hurried downstream, around the bend to where he could see the tank. The ugly relic gaped at him balefully from across the cut. Nothing moved, and there was only the sound of wind and the water.

"Bang!" cried a small voice.

The boy raised his head from the turret triumphantly. "Gotcha!" he said.

BLESSED
ARE THE
HAPPY-GO-LUCKY
GIRLS AND BOYS.

Brighten Up

There was a time when I was at one with my Father in feeling that to become a reverent, brave, trustworthy, and courteous Eagle Scout was to lay the foundations for a bountiful life. But I have since had occasion to reflect more realistically upon twig-bending, and am wondering now if Hell's Kitchen isn't a more sound preparation for living than was the Beaver Patrol. I cannot help feeling that my friend Louis Gigliano, who had been smoking cigars since he was twelve, was a great deal better prepared to thrive in chaos than was I, who had been trained to meet adversity with a combination pocketknife, can opener, and leather punch.

The test of the manly art of surviving I have in mind took place in a prisoner-of-war camp in Dresden. I, a clean-cut American youth, and Louis, a dissipated little weasel whose civilian occupation had been hashish-peddling to bobby-soxers, faced life there together. I am remembering Louis now because I am stone-broke, and because I know that Louis is living like a prince somewhere in this world he understands too well. It was that way in Germany.

Under the democratic provisions of the Geneva Convention, we, as privates, were obliged to work for our keep. All of us worked, that is, but Louis. His first act behind barbed wire was to report to an English-speaking Nazi guard that he wanted no part of the war, which he considered to be brother against brother, and the handiwork of Roosevelt and Jewish international bankers. I asked him if he meant it.

"I'm tired, for God's sake," he said. "I fought 'em for six months, and now I'm tired. I need a rest, and I like to eat as well as the next guy. Brighten up, will you!"

"I'd rather not, thank you," I said icily.

I was sent out on a pick-and-shovel detail; Louis remained in camp as the German sergeant's orderly. Louis got extra rations for whisk-brooming the sergeant three times a day. I got a hernia while tidying up after the American Air Force.

"Collaborationist!" I hissed at him after a particularly exhausting day in the streets. He was standing at the prison gate with a guard, immaculate and sprightly, nodding to his acquaintances in the dusty, weary column. His response to my taunt was to walk beside me to the sleeping quarters.

He laid a hand on my shoulder. "And then you can look at it this way, kid," he said. "Here you're helping Jerry clean up his streets so he can run tanks and trucks through 'em again. That's what I'd call collaboration. Me a collaborator?

You've got it backwards. All I do to help Jerry win the war is smoke his cigarettes and hit him for more to eat. That's bad, I suppose?"

I flopped down on my bunk. Louis took a seat on a straw-tick nearby. My arm hung over the side of the bunk, and Louis interested himself in my wrist watch, a gift from my Mother.

"Nice, very nice watch, kid," he said. And then, "Hungry after all that work, I'll bet."

I was ravenous. Ersatz coffee, one bowl of watered soup, and three slices of dry bread are not the sort of fare to delight a pick-swinger's heart after nine hours of hard labor. Louis was sympathetic. He liked me; he wanted to help. "You're a nice kid," he said. "I'll tell you what I'll do. I'll make a quick deal for you. There's no sense in going hungry. Why, that watch is worth two loaves of bread, at least. Is that a good deal, or isn't it?"

At that point, two loaves of bread was a dazzling lure. It was an incredible amount of food for one person to have. I tried to bid him up. "Look, friend," he said, "this is a special price to you, and it's a top price. I'm trying to do you a favor, see? All I ask of you is to keep quiet about this deal, or everybody will want two loaves for a watch. Promise?"

I swore by all that is holy that I would never reveal the magnanimity of Louis, my best friend. He was back in an hour. He cast a furtive glance around the room, withdrew a long loaf from a rolled field jacket, and stuffed it beneath my mattress. I waited for him to make the second deposit. It was not forthcoming. "I hardly know what to tell you, kid. The guard I do business with told me the whole bottom's dropped out of the watch market since all these guys came in from the Bulge. Too many watches all at one time is what did it. I'm sorry, but I want you to know that Louis got you the maximum for that watch." He made a move toward the loaf under the mattress. "If you feel gypped, all you have to do is say the word, and I'll take this back and get your watch again."

My stomach growled. "Oh hell, Louis," I sighed, "leave it there."

When I awoke the next morning, I looked at my wrist to see what time it was. And then I recalled that I no longer owned a watch. The man in the bunk overhead was also astir. I asked him for the time. He stuck his head over the side, and I saw that his jaws were crammed with bread; he blew a shower of crumbs over me as he answered. He said he no longer had a watch. He chewed and swallowed until a major portion of the great wad of bread was cleared from his mouth and he could make himself understood. "I should care what time it is when Louis will give me two loaves and ten cigarettes for a watch that wasn't worth twenty dollars new?" he asked.

Louis had a monopoly on rapport with the guards. His avowed harmony with Nazi principles convinced our keepers that he was the only bright one among us, and we all had to do our Black-Marketeering through this superficial Judas. Six weeks after we had been quartered in Dresden, nobody had any way of knowing what time it was outside of Louis and the guards. Two weeks after that, Louis had done every married man out of his wedding ring with this argument: "O.K., go ahead and be sentimental, go ahead and starve to death. Love's a wonderful thing, they tell me."

His profits were enormous. I later found out that my watch, for instance, brought a price of one hundred cigarettes and six loaves of bread. Anyone familiar with starvation will recognize that this was a handsome prize. Louis converted most of his wealth into the most negotiable of all securities, cigarettes. And it wasn't long before the possibilities of being a loan shark had occurred to him. Once every two weeks we were issued twenty cigarettes. Slaves of the tobacco habit would exhaust the ration in one or two days, and would be in a state of frenzy until the next ration came. Louis, who was coming to be known as "The People's Friend" or "Honest John," announced that cigarettes might be borrowed from him at a reasonable fifty-percent interest until the next ration. He soon had his wealth loaned out and increasing by half every two weeks. I was terribly in debt to him, with nothing left for collateral but my soul. I took him to task for his greed: "Christ drove the moneylenders from the temple," I reminded him.

"That was money they were lending, my boy," he replied. "I'm not beggin' you to borrow my cigarettes, am I? You're beggin' me to lend you some. Cigarettes are luxuries, friend. You don't have to smoke to stay alive. You'd probably live longer if you didn't smoke. Why don't you give up the filthy habit?"

"How many can you let me have until next Tuesday?" I asked.

When usury had swelled his hoard to an all-time high, a catastrophe, which he had been awaiting impatiently, caused the value of his cigarettes to sky-rocket. The USAAF swept over the feeble Dresden defenses to demolish, among other things, the major cigarette factories. As a consequence, not only the P.W. cigarette ration, but that of the guards and civilians as well, was cut off completely. Louis was a major figure in local finance. The guards found themselves without a smoke to their names, and began selling our rings and watches back to Louis at a lower price than they had given him. Some put his wealth as high as one hundred watches. Louis' own estimate, however, was a modest fifty-three watches, seventeen wedding rings, seven high school rings, and an heirloom watch-fob. "Some of the watches need a lot of work done on them," he told me.

When I say that the AAF got the cigarette factories among other things, I mean that a number of human beings got blown up as well—something like 200,000. Our activities took a ghoulish turn. We were put to work exhuming the dead from their innumerable crypts. Many of them wore jewelry, and most had carried their precious belongings to the shelters. At first we shunned the grave goods. For one thing, some of us felt that stripping corpses was a revolting business, and for another, to be caught at it was certain death. It took Louis to bring us to our senses. "Good God, kid, you could make enough to retire on in fifteen minutes. I just wish they'd let me go out with you guys for just a day." He licked his lips, and continued: "Tell you what—I'll really make it worth your while. You get me one good diamond ring, and I'll keep you in smokes and chow for as long as we're in this hole."

The next evening I brought him his ring, tucked into my trouser cuff. So, it turned out, did everyone else. When I showed him the diamond he shook his head. "Oh, what a dirty shame," he said. He held the stone up to a light: "Here the poor kid risked his life for a zircon!" Everybody, a minute inspection revealed, had brought back either a zircon, a garnet, or a paste diamond. In addition, Louis pointed out, any slight value these might have was destroyed because of a glutted market. I let my plunder go for four cigarettes; others got a bit of cheese, a few hundred grams of bread, or twenty potatoes. Some hung on to their gems. Louis chatted with them from time to time about the dangers of being caught with loot. "Poor devil over at the British Compound got it today," he would say. "They caught him with a pearl necklace sewed into his shirt. It only took 'em two hours to try him and shoot him." Sooner or later everyone made a deal with Louis.

Shortly after the last of us had been cleaned out, the S.S. came through our quarters on a surprise inspection. Louis' bed was the only one undisturbed. "He never leaves the compound and is a perfect prisoner," a guard was quick to explain to the inspectors. My mattress was slashed open and the straw scattered over the floor when I came home that evening.

However, Louis' luck was not air-tight, for in the last weeks of fighting, our guards were sent to stem the Russian tide, and a company of lame old men was moved in to watch over us. The new sergeant had no need for an orderly, and Louis sank into the anonymity of our group. The most humiliating aspect of his new situation was the prospect of being sent out on a labor detail with the common people. He was bitter about it, and demanded an interview with the new sergeant. He got the interview and was gone for about an hour.

When he got back I asked him, "Well, how much does Hitler want for Berchtesgaden?"

Louis was carrying a parcel wrapped in toweling. He opened it to reveal two pairs of scissors, some clippers, and a razor. "I'm the camp barber," he announced. "By order of the camp commandant, I am to make you gentlemen presentable."

"What if I don't want you to cut my hair?" I asked.

"Then you get your rations cut in half. That's by order of the commandant, too."

"Do you mind telling us how you got this appointment?" I asked.

"Not at all, not at all," said Louis. "I just told him I was ashamed to be associated with a bunch of sloppy men who look like gangsters, and that he ought to be ashamed to have such a terrible bunch in his prison. We two, the commandant and I, are going to do something about it." He set a stool in the middle of the floor and motioned me toward it. "You're first, kid," he said. "The commandant noticed those long locks of yours, and told me to be sure and get 'em."

I sat down on the stool and he whisked a towel around my neck. There was no mirror in which I could watch him cut, but his operations felt professional enough. I remarked on his unsuspected skill as a barber.

"Nothing, really," he said. "Sometimes I surprise myself." He finished with the clippers. "That will be two cigarettes, or the equivalent," he said. I paid him in saccharine tablets. No one but Louis had any cigarettes.

"Want a look at yourself?" He handed me a fragment of mirror. "Not bad, eh? And the best thing about it is that it's probably the worst job I'll do, because I'm bound to improve with time."

"Holy smokes!" I shrieked. My scalp looked like the back of an Airedale with mange—patches of bare scalp alternated with wild tufts of hair, and blood oozed from a dozen tiny cuts.

"Do you mean to say that for doing a job like this you get to stay in camp all day?" I roared.

"Come on, kid, simmer down," said Louis. "I think you look real nice."

There wasn't anything very novel about the situation after all. It was business as usual with him. The rest of us continued to work our heads off all day, and to come home weary in the evenings to be trimmed by Louis Gigliano.

IN THE U.S.A.
IT'S WINNERS
VS.
LOSERS,
AND THE FIX
IS
ON.

The Unicorn Trap

In the year 1067, *anno Domini,* in the village of Stow-on-the-Wold, England, eighteen dead men turned this way and that in the eighteen arches of the village gibbet. Hanged by Robert the Horrible, a friend of William the Conqueror, they boxed the compass with fishy eyes. North, east, south, west, and north again, there was no hope for the kind, the poor, and the thoughtful.

Across the road from the gibbet lived Elmer the woodcutter, his wife Ivy, and Ethelbert, his ten-year-old son.

Behind Elmer's hut was the forest.

Elmer closed the door of his hut, closed his eyes and licked his lips and tasted rue. He sat down at the table with Ethelbert. Their gruel had grown cold during the unexpected visit from the squire of Robert the Horrible.

Ivy pressed her back to the wall, as though God had just passed by. Her eyes were bright, her breathing shallow.

Ethelbert stared at his cold gruel blankly, bleakly, his young mind waterlogged in a puddle of family tragedy.

"Oh, didn't Robert the Horrible look grand, though, sitting out there on his horse?" said Ivy. "All that iron and paint and feathers, and such extra-fancy drapes on his horse." She flapped her rags and tossed her head like an empress as the hoofbeats of the Normans' horses died away.

"Grand, all right," said Elmer. He was a small man with a large-domed head. His blue eyes were restless with unhappy intelligence. His small frame was laced with scraggly ropes of muscle, the bonds of a thinking man forced to labor. "Grand is what he is," he said.

"You can say what you want about them Normans," said Ivy, "they done brought class to England."

"We're paying for it," said Elmer. "There's no such thing as a free lunch." He buried his fingers in the flaxen thatch of Ethelbert's hair, tilted the boy's head back, and searched his eyes for a sign that life was worth living. He saw only a mirror image of his own troubled soul.

"All the neighbors must of saw Robert the Horrible snarling out front, so high and mighty," said Ivy proudly. "Just wait till they hear he sent his squire in here to make you the new tax collector."

Elmer shook his head, his lips waggling slackly. He had lived to be loved for his wisdom and harmlessness. Now he had been told to represent Robert the Horrible's greed—or die horribly.

"I'd like to have me a dress made out of what his horse

was wearing," said Ivy. "Blue, all shot through with them little gold crosses." She was happy for the first time in her life. "I'd make it look careless-like," she said, "all kind of bunched up in back and dragging—only there wouldn't be nothing careless about it. And maybe, after I got me some decent clothes, I could pick me up a little French, and *parlee voo* with the Norman ladies, so refined and all."

Elmer sighed and cupped his son's hands in his own. Ethelbert's hands were coarse. The palms were scratched, and earth had worked into the pores and under the nails. Elmer traced a scratch with his fingertip. "How'd you get this?" he said.

"Working on the trap," said Ethelbert. He came to life, radiant with intelligence of his own. "I been fixing thorn trees over the hole," he said eagerly, "so when the unicorn falls in, the thorn trees fall in on top of him."

"That should hold him," said Elmer tenderly. "It isn't many families in England that can look forward to a unicorn dinner."

"I wish you'd come up in the forest and have a look at the trap," said Ethelbert. "I want to make sure I got it right."

"I'm sure it's a fine trap, and I *want* to see it," said Elmer. The dream of catching a unicorn ran through the drab fabric of the lives of the father and son like a golden thread.

Both knew there were no unicorns in England. But they'd agreed to madness—to live as though there were unicorns around; as though Ethelbert were going to catch one any day; as though the scrawny family would soon be stuffing itself with meat, selling the precious horn for a fortune, living happily ever after.

"You've been saying you'd come and see it for a year," said Ethelbert.

"I've been busy," said Elmer. He didn't want to inspect the trap, to see it for what it really was—a handful of twigs over a scratch in the ground, magnified into a great engine of hope by the boy's imagination. Elmer wanted to go on thinking of it as big and promising, too. There was no hope anywhere else.

Elmer kissed his son's hands, and sniffed the mingled smells of flesh and earth. "I'll come see it soon," he said.

"And I'd have enough left over from them horse drapes to make drawers for you and little Ethelbert," said Ivy, still enchanted. "Wouldn't you two be the ones, though, with blue drawers all shot through with them little gold crosses?"

"Ivy," said Elmer patiently, "I wish you'd get it through your head—Robert really *is* horrible. He isn't going to give you the drapes off his horse. He never gave anybody *any*thing."

"I guess I can dream if I want to," said Ivy. "I guess that's a woman's privilege."

"Dream of what?" said Elmer.

"If you do a good job, he just *might* give me the drapes

off his horse after they're all wore out," said Ivy. "And maybe, if you collect so many taxes they can't hardly believe it, maybe they'll invite us to the castle sometimes." She walked about the hut coquettishly, holding the hem of an imaginary train above the dirt floor. *"Bon joor, monsoor, madame,"* she said. "I trust your lordship and ladyship ain't poorly."

"Is that the best dream you've got?" said Elmer, shocked.

"And they'd give you some distinguished name like Elmer the Bloody or Elmer the Mad," said Ivy, "and you and me and Ethelbert would ride to church on Sundays, all spruced up, and if some old serf talked to us snotty, we'd haul off and—"

"Ivy!" cried Elmer. "We *are* serfs."

Ivy tapped her foot and rocked her head from side to side. "Ain't Robert the Horrible just gave us the opportunity to improve ourselves?" she said.

"To be as bad as *he* is?" said Elmer. "That's an improvement?"

Ivy sat down at the table, and put her feet up on it. "If a body gets stuck in the ruling classes through no fault of their own," she said, "they got to rule or have folks just lose all respect for government." She scratched herself daintily. "Folks got to be governed."

"To their sorrow," said Elmer.

"Folks got to be protected," said Ivy, "and armor and castles don't come cheap."

Elmer rubbed his eyes. "Ivy, would you tell me what it is we're being protected from that's so much worse than what we've got?" he said. "I'd like to have a look at it, and then make up my own mind about what scares me most."

Ivy wasn't listening to him. She was thrilling to the approach of hoofbeats. Robert the Horrible and his entourage passed on their way back to the castle, and the hut trembled with might and glory.

Ivy ran to the door and threw it open.

Elmer and Ethelbert bowed their heads.

There were shouts of happy surprise from the Normans.

"Hien!"

"Regardez!"

"Donnez la chasse, mes braves!"

The Normans' horses reared, wheeled, and galloped into the forest.

"What's the good news?" said Elmer. "Did they squash something?"

"They seen a deer!" said Ivy. "They're all taking out after it, with Robert the Horrible in front." She put her hand over her heart. "Ain't he the sportsman, though?"

"Ain't he, though," said Elmer. "May God make his right arm strong." He looked to Ethelbert for an answering sardonic smile.

Ethelbert's thin face was white. His eyes bugged. "The trap—they're going up where the trap is!" he said.

"If they lay a finger on that trap," said Elmer, "I'll—"
The cords in his neck stood out and his hands became
claws. Of course Robert the Horrible would hack the boy's
work of love to pieces if he saw it. *"Pour le sport, pour le
sport,"* he said bitterly.

Elmer tried to daydream of murdering Robert the
Horrible, but the dream was as frustrating as life—a search
for weaknesses where there were no weaknesses. The dream
ended truthfully, with Robert and his men on horses as
big as cathedrals, with Robert and his men in iron shells,
laughing behind the bars of their visors, choosing at leisure
from their collections of skewers, chains, hammers, and
meat-axes—choosing ways to deal with an angry wood-
cutter in rags.

Elmer's hands went limp. "If they wreck the trap," he
said flabbily, "we'll build another one, better than ever."

Shame for his weakness made Elmer sick. The sickness
worsened. He rested his head on his folded arms. When he
raised his head, it was to look about himself with a death's-
head grin. He had passed his breaking point.

"Father! Are you all right?" said Ethelbert, alarmed.

Elmer stood shakily. "Fine," he said, "just fine."

"You look so different," said Ethelbert.

"I *am* different," said Elmer. "I'm not afraid anymore."
He gripped the edge of the table and shouted. "I'm not
afraid!"

"Hush!" said Ivy. "They'll hear you!"

"I will *not* hush!" said Elmer passionately.

"You better hush," said Ivy. "You know what Robert the Horrible does to people who won't hush."

"Yes," said Elmer, "he nails their hats to their heads. But, if that's the price I have to pay, I'll pay it." He rolled his eyes. "When I thought of Robert the Horrible wrecking the boy's trap, the *whole story of life* came to me in a blinding flash!"

"Father, listen—" said Ethelbert, "I'm not scared he's going to wreck the trap. I'm scared he's going to—"

"A blinding flash!" cried Elmer.

"Oh, for crying out loud," said Ivy impatiently, closing the door. "All right, all right, all right," she said with a sigh, "let's hear the story of life in a blinding flash."

Ethelbert tugged at his father's sleeve. "If I do say so myself," he said, "that trap is a—"

"The wreckers against the builders!" said Elmer. "There's the whole story of life!"

Ethelbert shook his head and talked to himself. "If his horse ever steps on the rope that's hooked up to the sapling that's hooked up to the—" He bit his lip.

"Are you all through, Elmer?" said Ivy. "Is that it?" Her eagerness to get back to watching the Normans was infuriatingly transparent. He fingered the doorpull.

"No, Ivy," said Elmer tensely, "I am *not* through." He knocked her hand away from the doorpull.

"You done struck me," said Ivy, amazed.

"All day you have that thing open!" said Elmer. "I wish we didn't have a door! All day you do nothing but sit in front of the door, watching executions and waiting for the Normans to pass." He shivered his hands in her face. "No wonder your brains are all fuddled with glory and violence!"

Ivy cringed pitifully. "I just watch," she said. "A body gets lonely, and it helps to make the time go."

"You've been watching too long!" said Elmer. "And I've got more news for you."

"Yes?" piped Ivy.

Elmer squared his narrow shoulders. "Ivy," he said, "I am not going to be tax collector for Robert the Horrible."

Ivy gasped.

"I am not going to help the wreckers," said Elmer. "My son and I are builders."

"He'll hang you if you don't," said Ivy. "He promised he would."

"I know," said Elmer. "I know." Fear hadn't come to him yet. Pain hadn't come where pain would come. There was only the feeling of having done something perfect at last— the taste of a drink from a cold, pure spring.

Elmer opened the door. The wind had freshened, and the chains by which the dead men hung sang a chorus of slow, rusty squawks. The wind came from over the forest, and it carried to Elmer's ears the cries of the Norman sportsmen.

The cries sounded strangely bewildered, unsure. Elmer supposed that this was because they were so far away.

"*Robert? Allo, allo? Robert? Hien! Allo, allo?*"

"*Allo? Allo? Hien! Robert—dites quelque chose, s'il vous plaît. Hien! Hien! Allo?*"

"*Allo, allo, allo? Robert? Robert l'horrible? Hien! Allo, allo, allo?*"

Ivy put her arms around Elmer from behind, and rested her cheek on his back. "Elmer, honey," she said, "I don't want you to get hung. I love you, honey."

Elmer patted her hands. "And I love you, Ivy," he said. "I'll miss you."

"You're really going through with it?" said Ivy.

"It's time to die for what I believe in," said Elmer. "And even if it wasn't, I'd still have to."

"Why, why?" said Ivy.

"Because I said I would in front of my son," said Elmer. Ethelbert came to him, and Elmer put his arms around the boy.

The little family was now bound by a tangle of arms. The three entwined rocked back and forth as the sun set—rocked in a rhythm they felt in their bones.

Ivy sniffled against Elmer's back. "You're just teaching Ethelbert how to get *his* self hung, too," she said. "He's so fresh with them Normans now, it's a wonder they ain't flang him down the oubliette."

"I only hope that Ethelbert has a son like mine before he dies," said Elmer.

"Everything seemed to be going so grand," said Ivy. She burst into tears. "Here you was offered a fine position, with a chance for advancement," she said brokenly. "And I figured maybe, after Robert the Horrible had wore out his horse drapes, you could kind of ask him—"

"Ivy!" said Elmer. "Don't make me feel worse. Comfort me."

"It'd be a sight easier, if I knew what it was you thought you was doing," said Ivy.

Two Normans came out of the forest, unhappy and baffled. They faced each other, spread their arms, and shrugged.

One pushed a shrub aside with his broadsword and looked under it pathetically. *"Allo, allo?"* he said. *"Robert?"*

"Il a disparu!" said the other.

"Il s'est évanoui!"

"Le cheval, l'armement, les plumes—tout d'un coup!"

"Poof!"

"Hélas!"

They saw Elmer and his family. *"Hien!"* called one to Elmer. *"Avez-vous vu Robert?"*

"Robert the Horrible?" said Elmer.

"Oui."

"Sorry," said Elmer. "Haven't seen hide nor hair of him."

"Eh?"

"Je n'ai vu pas ni peau ni cheveux de lui," said Elmer.

The Normans faced each other again, desolately.

"Hélas!"

"Zut!"

They went into the forest again slowly.

"Allo, allo, allo?"

"Hien! Robert? Allo?"

"Father! Listen!" said Ethelbert wildly.

"Shhhhh," said Elmer gently. "I'm talking to your mother now."

"It's just like that fool unicorn trap," said Ivy. "I didn't understand that, neither. I was real patient about that trap. I never said a word. But now I'm going to speak my piece."

"Speak it," said Elmer.

"That trap don't have nothing to do with nothing," said Ivy.

Tears formed on the rims of Elmer's eyes. The image of the twigs, the scratch in the earth, and the boy's imagination said all there was to say about his life—the life that was about to end.

"There ain't no unicorns around here," said Ivy, proud of her knowledge.

"I know," said Elmer. "Ethelbert and I know."

"And you getting yourself hung ain't going to make anything better, neither," said Ivy.

"I know. Ethelbert and I know that, too," said Elmer.

"Maybe *I'm* the dumb one," said Ivy.

Elmer suddenly felt the terror and loneliness and pain-to-come that were the price for the perfect thing he was doing—the price of the taste of a drink from a cold, pure spring. They were far worse than shame could ever be.

Elmer swallowed. His neck hurt where the noose would bite. "Ivy, honey," he said, "I sure *hope* you are."

That night, Elmer prayed for a new husband for Ivy, a stout heart for Ethelbert, and a merciful death and paradise for himself on the morrow.

"Amen," said Elmer.

"Maybe you could just *pretend* to be tax collector," said Ivy.

"Where would I get the just-pretend taxes?" said Elmer.

"Maybe you could be tax collector for just a little while," said Ivy.

"Just long enough to get hated for good reason," said Elmer. "*Then* I could hang."

"There's always something," said Ivy. Her nose reddened.

"Ivy—" said Elmer.

"Hmmm?"

"Ivy—I understand about the blue dress all shot through with little gold crosses," said Elmer. "I want that for you, too."

"And the drawers for you and Ethelbert," said Ivy. "It wasn't all just for me."

"Ivy," said Elmer, "what I'm doing—it's more important than those horse drapes."

"That's my trouble," said Ivy. "I just can't imagine anything grander than them."

"Neither can I," said Elmer. "But there are such things. There's *got* to be." He smiled sadly. "Whatever they are," he said, "they're what I'll be dancing about when I dance on air tomorrow."

"I wish Ethelbert would get back," said Ivy. "We should all be together."

"He had to check his trap," said Elmer. "Life goes on."

"I'm glad them Normans finally went home," said Ivy. "It was *allo* and *hien* and *hélas* and *zut* and *poof* till I thought I'd near go crazy. I guess they done found Robert the Horrible."

"Thus sealing my doom," said Elmer. He sighed. "I'll go look for Ethelbert," he said. "How better could a man spend his last night on earth than in bringing his son home from the forest?"

Elmer went out into a pale blue world of night under a half-moon. He followed the path that Ethelbert's feet had worn—followed it to the high, black wall of the forest.

"Ethelbert!" he called.

There was no reply.

Elmer pushed into the forest. Branches whipped his face, and brambles snatched at his legs.

"Ethelbert!"

Only the gibbet replied. The chains squawked, and a skeleton fell rattling to earth. There were now only seventeen exhibits in the eighteen arches. There was room for one more.

Elmer's anxiety for Ethelbert grew. It drove him hard, deeper and deeper into the forest. He came to a clearing, and rested, panting, sweat stinging his eyes.

"Ethelbert!"

"Father?" said Ethelbert in the thicket ahead. "Come here and help me."

Elmer went into the thicket blindly, his hands groping before him.

Ethelbert caught his father's hand in the perfect darkness. "Careful!" said Ethelbert. "Another step, and you'll be in the trap."

"Oh," said Elmer. "*That* was a close thing." Playfully, to make the boy feel good, he filled his voice with fear. "Whoooooey! I *guess!*"

Ethelbert pulled his hand down, and pressed it against something lying on the ground.

Elmer was amazed to feel the form of a big, dead stag. He knelt by it. "A deer!" he said.

His voice came back to him, seemingly from the bowels of the earth. *"A deer, a deer, a deer."*

"It took me an hour to get it out of the trap," said Ethelbert.

"Trap, trap, trap," said the echo.

"Really?" said Elmer. "Good Lord, boy! I had no idea that trap was that good!"

"Good, good, good," said the echo.

"You don't know the half of it," said Ethelbert.

"It, it, it," said the echo.

"Where's that echo coming from?" said Elmer.

"From, from, from?" said the echo.

"From right in front of you," said Ethelbert. "From the trap."

Elmer threw himself backwards as Ethelbert's voice came out of the hole before him, came out of the earth as though from the gates of Hell itself.

"Trap, trap, trap."

"You *dug* it?" said Elmer, aghast.

"God dug it," said Ethelbert. "It's the chimney of a cave."

Elmer stretched out limp on the ground. He rested his head on the cooling, stiffening haunch of the stag. There was only one flaw in the thicket's roof of verdure. Through that flaw came the light from one bright star. Elmer saw the star as a rainbow through the prisms of grateful tears.

"I have nothing more to ask of life," said Elmer. "Tonight, everything has been given me—and more, and more, and more. With God's help, my son has caught a unicorn." He touched Ethelbert's foot, and stroked its arch. "If God listens even to the prayers of an humble wood-cutter and his son," he said, "what *can't* the world become?"

Elmer almost slipped away to sleep, so much at one was he with the plan of things.

Ethelbert roused him. "Shall we take the stag down to Mom?" said Ethelbert. "A midnight feast?"

"Not the whole deer," said Elmer. "Too risky. We'll cut some choice steaks, and leave the rest hidden here."

"Have you got a knife?" said Ethelbert.

"No," said Elmer. "Against the law, you know."

"I'll get something to cut with," said Ethelbert.

Elmer, still lying down, heard his son lower himself into the chimney of the cave; heard him seek and find footholds deeper and deeper in the earth; heard him grunting and wrestling with logs at the bottom.

When Ethelbert returned, he was carrying something long that caught the glint from the one bright star. "This should do it," he said.

He gave to Elmer Robert the Horrible's keen, two-handed broadsword.

It was midnight.

The little family was stuffed with venison.

Elmer picked his teeth with Robert the Horrible's poignard.

Ethelbert, on watch at the door, wiped his lips with a plume.

Ivy pulled the horse-drapes about her contentedly. "If I'd of knowed you was going to catch something," she said, "I wouldn't of thought that trap was such a dumb idea."

"That's the way it is with traps," said Elmer. He leaned back and tried to feel elated about not hanging the next day, now that Robert the Horrible was dead. But he found the reprieve a dull affair compared to the other thoughts carousing in the stately dome of his head.

"There's just one thing I got to ask," said Ivy.

"Name it," said Elmer expansively.

"I wish you two'd quit making light of me, telling me this is unicorn meat," said Ivy. "You think I'll believe anything you tell me."

"It *is* unicorn meat," said Elmer. "And I'm going to tell you something else you can believe." He slipped on Robert the Horrible's iron gauntlet, and rapped the table with it. "Ivy—there's a great day coming for the little people."

Ivy looked at him adoringly. "Ain't you and Ethelbert nice," she said, "going out and getting me the clothes for it?"

There were hoofbeats in the distance.

"Hide everything!" said Ethelbert.

In an instant, every vestige of Robert the Horrible and the deer was out of sight.

Norman warriors, armed to the teeth, thundered by Elmer the woodcutter's humble hut.

They shouted in fear and defiance of formless demons in the night.

"Hien! Hien! Courage, mes braves!"

The hoofbeats faded away.

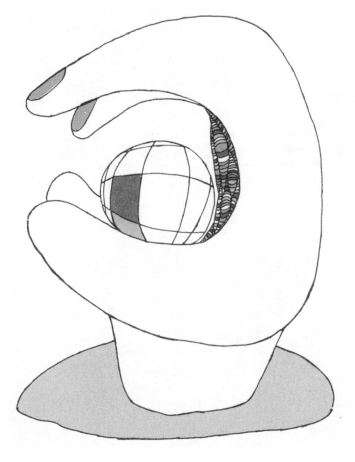

 Unknown Soldier

It was all nonsense, of course, when they said our baby was the first one to be born in New York City into the third millennium of the Christian era—at ten seconds past midnight on January first, 2000. For starters, the third millennium, as countless people had pointed out, would not begin until January first, 2001. Planetarily speaking, the new year was already six hours old when our child was born, since it had begun that much earlier at the Royal Observatory in Greenwich, England, where time begins. Never mind that the numbering of years since the birth of Christ could only be approximate. The datum was so obscure. And who can say in which minute a child was born? When its head appeared? When all of it was outside the mother? When the umbilical cord was cut? Since there were many valuable prizes to be given to the city's first baby of 2000, and its parents, and the chief physician in attendance, it was agreed well in advance of the contest that severing the cord should not count, since the moment could be delayed past the crucial midnight. There might be doctors all over the city with their eyes on the clock and their scissors poised, and of course with witnesses present, watching the scissors, watching the clock. The winning doctor would get an all-expense-paid vacation on one of the few islands where a tourist could still feel fairly secure, which was Bermuda. A battalion of British paratroops was stationed there. Understandably, doctors might be tempted to fudge the birthtime, given the opportunity.

No matter what the criteria, defining the moment of birth was a lot less controversial than declaring when a fertilized ovum was a human being in the mother's womb. For the purpose of the contest, the moment of birth was the moment when the baby's eyes or eyelids were first bathed in light from the outside world, when they could first be seen by the witnesses. So the baby, which was the case with ours, would still be partly inside the mother. If she had been a breech-birth, of course, the eyes would have been almost the last things to appear. And here comes the most nonsensical aspect of the contest we won: If she had been a breech-birth, or had Down's syndrome or spina bifida or been a crack baby or an AIDS baby or whatever, she surely would have been disqualified for the prizes on some supposed technicality having to do with timing rather than, or so the judges would have said, her variations from so-called norms. She was, after all, supposed to symbolize how healthy and delightful the next thousand years were supposed to be.

One guarantee by the judges was that race and religion and national origin of the parents could not possibly skew their deliberations. And it is true that I am a native American Black, and my wife, while classified as white, was born in Cuba. But it surely did not hurt that I was head of the Sociology Department at Columbia University, or that my wife was a physical therapist at New York Hospital. I am certain that our baby won over several other candidates, including a newborn boy found in a trashcan in Brooklyn, because we were middle class.

We got a Ford station wagon and three lifetime passes to Disney World and a home entertainment console, with a six-foot screen and a VCR and a sound system capable of playing every sort of record or tape, and equipment for a home gymnasium, and so on. And the baby got a Government Bond worth fifty thousand dollars at maturity, and a bassinet and a stroller and free diaper service and on and on. But then she died when she was only six weeks old. The doctor who helped her into the world was in Bermuda at the time, and he did not hear about her death there. Her death was no more big news there, or anywhere outside of New York City, than her birth had been. It wasn't big news here, either, since nobody but the promoters of the asinine contest and the business people who had donated the prizes took all the hoopla about her at all seriously, the blather about her representing so many wonderful things, the mingling of races in beauty and happiness, the rebirth of the spirit which had once made New York the greatest city in the world in the greatest nation in the world, and just plain peace, and I don't know what all. It seems to me now that she was like an unknown soldier in a war memorial, a little bit of flesh and bone and hair which was extolled to the point of lunacy. Hardly anybody came to her funeral, incidentally. The TV station whose idea the contest was sent a minor executive, not even a personality, and surely not a camera crew. Who wants to watch the burial of the next thousand years? If television refuses to look at something, it is as though it never happened. It can erase anything, even whole continents, such as Africa, one big desert now, where millions upon millions of babies, with a brand-new thousand years of history looming before them, starve to death. It was Crib Death Syndrome which killed our daughter, they say. This is a genetic defect as yet, and perhaps forever, undetectable by amniocentesis. She was our first child. Ah me.

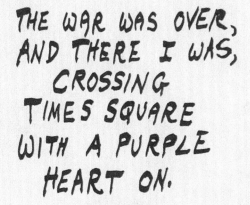

THE WAR WAS OVER,
AND THERE I WAS,
CROSSING
TIMES SQUARE
WITH A PURPLE
HEART ON.

Spoils

If, on Judgment Day, God were to ask Paul which of the two should rightly be his eternal residence, Heaven or Hell, Paul would likely suggest that, by his own and by Cosmic standards, Hell was his destiny—recalling the wretched thing he had done. The Almighty, in all His Wisdom, might recognize that Paul's life on the whole had been a harmless one, and that his tender conscience had already tortured him mightily—for the thing he did.

Paul's garish adventures as a prisoner of war in Sudetenland lost their troubling forms as they mired down in the past, but one dismal image would not sink from his consciousness. His wife's playful banter at dinner one night served to recall what he longed to forget. Sue had spent the afternoon with Mrs. Ward, next door, and Mrs. Ward had shown her an exquisite silver service for twenty-four, which, Sue was astonished to learn, Mr. Ward had liberated and brought home from the war in Europe.

"Honey," Sue chided him, "couldn't you have brought home just a little something better than you did?"

It was not likely that the Germans bewailed Paul's plundering, for one rusty and badly bent Luftwaffe saber was the whole of his loot. His companions in the Russian Zone, under post-war anarchy, Free Enterprise *par excellence* that lasted for weeks, came home laden with treasure like Spanish galleons, while Paul was content with his foolish relic. Though he had weeks to seek and take what he would, his first hours as a swashbuckling conqueror were his last. The thing that broke his spirit and his hate, the image that tormented him, began taking shape on a glorious morning of Spring in the mountains, May 8, 1945.

It took Paul and his fellow prisoners of war in Hellendorf, Sudetenland, some time to get used to the absence of their guards, who had prudently taken to the forests and hilltops the night before. He and two other Americans wandered uncertainly down the teeming road toward Peterswald, another tranquil farming village of five hundred war-bewildered souls. Humanity moved in wailing rivers, flowing in both directions with a unanimous lament— "The Russians are coming!" After four tedious kilometers in this milieu, the three settled on the bank of a stream that cut through Peterswald, wondering how they might reach the American lines, wondering if the Russians were killing everyone in their path as some said. Near them, secure in a barn-sheltered hutch, a white rabbit sat in darkness, listening to the uncustomary din without.

The trio felt no part of the terror that surged through the village, no pity. "God knows the arrogant block-heads have been begging for it," said Paul, and the others nodded in grim amusement. "After what the Germans did to them, you can't blame the Russians, no matter what they do," said Paul; and again his companions nodded. They sat in silence and watched as frantic mothers hid with their young in cellars, as others scurried up the hillside and into the woods, or deserted their homes to flee down the road with a few precious parcels.

A wide-eyed, long-striding British lance corporal shouted from the road, "Better get a move on, lads; they're in Hellendorf right now!"

A cloud of dust in the west, the roar of trucks, the scattering of frightened refugees, and the Russians entered the village, pitching cigarettes to the astonished citizens, and giving wet, enthusiastic kisses to all who dared show themselves. Paul cavorted about their trucks, laughing and shouting, and catching the loaves and chunks of meat thrown to him by those liberators who heard his "American! American!" above the wild accordion music that streamed from the red-starred trucks. Happy and excited, he and his friends returned to the brookside with armloads of food, and at once began to stuff themselves.

But as they ate, the others—Czechs, Poles, Jugoslavs, Russians, a fearsome horde of outraged German slaves—came to smash and loot and burn for the merry hell of it, in the wake of the Russian Army. Systematically, in purposeful knots of three and four, they went from house to house, breaking down doors, threatening the occupants, and taking what pleased them. Overlooking plunder was not likely, for Peterswald was built in a narrow draw, only one house deep on either side of a single road. Paul thought that thousands must have explored every house from cellar to attic before the moonlit evening came.

He and his friends watched the earnest pillagers at work, giving them sickly smiles whenever a group passed by. An exultant pair of Scotchmen had made friends with such a group, and, while on a cheerful foray, stopped off to talk with the Americans. Each had a handsome bicycle, numerous rings and watches, field glasses, cameras, and other admirable trinkets.

"After all," one of them explained, "you don't want to be sittin' down on a day like this, you'll never get another chance like this one. You're the victors, you know, you've a bloody good right to anything you like."

The three Americans talked it up among themselves, Paul at the fore, and convinced each other that they would be completely justified in looting the homes of the enemy. The three together beset the nearest house, one which had been vacant since before their arrival in Peterswald. It had already been well-exploited; no glass remained in the windows; every drawer had been dumped, every garment torn from the closets; cupboards had been stripped bare, and pillows and mattresses had been disemboweled by searchers. Each of the marauders before Paul and his friends had examined the heaps discarded by his predecessor until nothing but shreds of cloth and a few pots remained.

It was nearly evening when they picked over the sorry lot, and they found nothing to interest them. Paul remarked that there probably was not much in the house to begin with; whoever had lived there had been poor. The furnishings were shabby, the walls peeling, and the outside in need of painting and repair. But when Paul climbed the stairway to the tiny upper floor, he found an amazing room that did not fit into the impoverished pattern. It was a bedroom decorated in gay colors, with beautifully carved furniture, fairyland pictures on candy-striped walls, and freshly painted woodwork. Discarded loot, a forlorn hillock of toys stood in the middle of the floor. The only undisturbed objects in the whole house, leaning against the wall near the head of the bed, were a pair of, "I'll be damned; look, kids' crutches."

The Americans, having found nothing of value, agreed that it was getting too late for treasure hunting that day, and proposed that they set about getting supper. They had a good quantity of food on hand that the Russians had given to them, but got the idea that supper on this day of days should certainly be something special, with chicken, milk, and eggs, and maybe even a rabbit. Seeking such delicacies, the trio broke up to scour the neighboring barns and farmyards.

Paul peered into the small barn behind the house which they had hoped to plunder. Whatever food or livestock may have been here had been carted east hours ago, he reflected. On the dirt floor near the doorway were a few potatoes which he picked up, but nothing else. As he stuffed the potatoes into his pockets and prepared to move on, he heard a slight rustling from one corner. The gentle noise was repeated. When his eyes became accustomed to the darkness he could see a rabbit hutch in which a fat, white rabbit sat, twinkling his pink nose and breathing quickly. This was sensational luck, the *pièce de résistance* for the banquet. Paul opened the door and removed the unprotesting animal, holding it by its ears. Never having killed a rabbit with his hands, he was dubious as to how he might do it. At last he laid the rabbit's head on a chopping block and smashed its skull with the back of an axe. It kicked feebly for a few seconds and died.

Delighted with himself, Paul set about skinning and cleaning the rabbit, cutting off a foot for good luck in surely better days to come. Finished, he stood in the barn doorway, contemplating peace, the sunset, and the stream of sheepish German soldiers shuffling home from the last pocket of resistance. With them were the weary civilians who had fled down the road that morning, only to be turned back by the Russian advance.

Suddenly Paul was aware of three figures who detached themselves from the dismal procession and moved toward him. They paused before the battered house. A wave of remorse and sorrow billowed in Paul's chest: "This must be their little house and barn," he thought. "This must belong to that old man and woman, and to that crippled boy." The woman wept and the man shook his head. The boy kept trying to get their attention, saying something and gesturing toward the barn. Paul stood in the shadows so they could not see him, and he ran away with the rabbit when they went into the house.

He brought his contribution to the place that the others had chosen for a fireplace, a knoll from which Paul could see the barn he had left through a gap in a poplar windbreak. The rabbit was placed with the rest of the booty on a cloth stretched over the ground.

As the others busied themselves with preparing the food, he watched the barn, for the little boy had come out of his house, and was moving toward the barn as swiftly as his crutches would carry him. He disappeared into the barn for an agonizing long time. Paul heard his faint shriek, and saw him come to the door, carrying the soft white pelt with him. He rubbed it against his cheek, and then sank to the doorsill to bury his face in the fur and sob his heart out.

Paul looked away, and did not look again. The other two did not see the child, and Paul did not tell them about him. When the three sat down to supper, one boy began grace: "Our Father, we thank thee for this food thou hast set before us . . ."

Heading for the American lines, moving casually from one village to the next, Paul's companions accumulated a sizeable quantity of German treasure. For some reason, all that Paul brought home was one rusty and badly bent Luftwaffe saber.

$\frac{1}{100}$ "TRUST ME."

Just You and Me, Sammy

I.

This story is about soldiers, but it isn't exactly a war story. The war was over when it all happened, so I guess that makes it a murder story. No mystery, just murder.

My name is Sam Kleinhans. It's a German name, and, I'm sorry to say, my father was mixed up in the *German-American Bund* in New Jersey for a while before the war. When he found out what it was all about, he got out in a hurry. But a lot of the people in our neighborhood went for the *Bund* in a big way. A couple of families on our street, I remember, got so excited about what Hitler was doing in the Fatherland, they sold everything they had, and went back to Germany to live.

Some of their kids were just about my age, and, when the U.S. got into the war and I went overseas as a rifleman, I wondered if I might not wind up shooting at some of my old playmates. I don't think I did. I found out afterwards that most of the *Bund* kids who took out German citizenship wound up as riflemen on the Russian front. A few got into small-time intelligence work, trying to mix in with American troops without being noticed, but not many. The Germans didn't trust them worth a damn—or at least that's what one of our former neighbors told Father in a letter asking him for a CARE parcel. The same man said he'd do anything to get back to the States, and I imagine they all feel that way.

Being so close to them and the *Bund* monkey business made me pretty self-conscious about my German ancestry when we finally got into the war. I must have seemed like quite a jerk to a lot of the guys, sounding off the way I did about loyalty, fighting for a cause, and all that. Not that the other guys in the Army didn't believe in those things—it's just that it wasn't fashionable to talk about them. Not in World War II.

Thinking back on it, I *know* I was corny. I remember what I said on the morning of May eighth, for instance, the day the war with Germany ended. "Isn't it glorious!" I said.

"Ain't what glorious?" said Private George Fisher, raising one eyebrow, as though he'd said something pretty deep. He was scratching his back on a strand of barbed-wire, thinking about something else, I guess. Food and cigarettes, probably, and maybe even women.

It wasn't very smart to be seen talking with George anymore. He didn't have any friends left in camp, and anybody who tried to be buddies with him was likely to wind up in the same lonely spot. All of us were milling around, and

George and I just happened—I thought then—to come together there by the gate.

The Germans had made him head American in our prison camp. They said it was because he could speak German. At any rate, he made a good thing out of it. He was a lot fatter than the rest of us—so he probably was thinking about women. Nobody else had mentioned the subject since about a month after we'd been captured. Everybody but George had been living on potatoes for eight months, so, like I said, the subject of women was about as popular as the subject of raising orchids or playing the zither.

The way I felt then, if Betty Grable had showed up and said she was all mine, I would have told her to make me a peanut butter and jelly sandwich. Only it wasn't Betty that was on her way to see George and me that day—it was the Russian Army. The two of us, standing on the road shoulder in front of the prison gate, were listening to the tanks whining in the valley, just starting to climb up to where we were.

The big guns to the north, that had been rattling the prison windowpanes for a week, were quiet now, and our guards had disappeared during the night. Before that, the only traffic on the road had been a few farmers' carts. Now it was packed with jostling, yelling people—pushing, stumbling, swearing; trying to cross the hills to Prague before the Russians caught them.

Fear like that can spread, too, to people who don't have anything to be afraid of. All of the people running from the Russians weren't Germans. I remember a British lance corporal, for instance, who George and I saw strutting toward Prague as though the Devil was after him.

"Better get a move on, Yanks!" he puffed. "Rooskies only a couple of miles back, you know. Don't want to mix it with them, do you?"

One nice thing about being half-starved, which I gather the lance corporal wasn't, is that it's hard to worry about anything but being half-starved. "You've got it all wrong, Mac," I shouted back at him. "We're on their side, the way I understand it."

"They're not asking where you're from, Yank. They're shooting everything they can catch for the fun of it." He rounded the bend and was out of sight.

I laughed, but I was in for a surprise when I turned back to George. He was running his stubby fingers through his red mop of hair, and his fat moon face was white as he looked down the road in the direction the Russians would be coming from. That was something none of us had ever seen before—George afraid.

Until then, he'd been in command of every situation, whether it was with us or with the Germans. He had a thick skin, and he could bluff or wheedle his way out of anything.

Alvin York would have been impressed with some of his

combat stories. We were all from the same division, except for George. He'd been brought in all by himself, and he said he'd been up front since D-Day. The rest of us were from a green outfit, captured in a breakthrough before we'd been in the line a week. George was a real campaigner, and entitled to a lot of respect. He got it; begrudged, all right, but he got it—until Jerry got killed.

"Call me a stool pigeon again, buddy, and I'll smash your ugly face in," I heard him tell one guy whose whispers he'd overheard. "You know damn well you'd do the same thing, if you had the chance. I'm just playing the guards for chumps. They think I'm on their side, so they treat me pretty good. I'm not hurting you none, so mind your own damn business!"

That was a few days after the break, after Jerry Sullivan got killed. Somebody'd tipped off the guards about the break, or at least it looked that way. They were waiting outside the fence, at the mouth of the tunnel, when Jerry, the first man through, crawled out. They didn't have to shoot him, but they did. Maybe George hadn't told the guards— but nobody gave him the benefit of that doubt when he was out of hearing.

Nobody said anything to his face. He was big and healthy, remember, and went on getting beefier and worse-tempered, while the rest of us were turning into drowsy scarecrows.

But now, with the Russians on their way, George's nerve seemed to have given out. "Let's make a break for Prague, Sammy. Just you and me, so we can travel fast," he said.

"What in hell's the matter with you?" I said. "We don't have to run from anybody, George. We just won a war, and you're acting like we lost one. Prague's sixty miles away, for God's sake. The Russians'll be here in an hour or so, and they'll probably send trucks to run us back to our lines. Take it easy, George—you don't hear any shooting, do you?"

"They'll shoot us, Sammy, sure as hell. You don't even look like an American soldier. They're wild men, Sammy. Come on, let's go while we got the chance."

He had a point about my clothes. They were ripped and stained and patched, and I looked more like a resident of skid row than an American soldier. But, as you might expect, George still looked pretty sharp. The guards kept him in cigarettes as well as food, and he could trade the smokes for just about anything in camp he wanted. He got himself several changes of clothes that way, and the guards let him use an iron they had in their shack, so he was the camp fashion plate.

His game was over now. Nobody had to trade with him anymore, and the men who'd taken such good care of him were gone. Maybe that's what was scaring him, and not the Russians. "Let's go, Sammy," he said. He was pleading with me, a person he hadn't had a friendly word for in eight months at close quarters.

"Go ahead, if you want to," I said. "You don't have to ask my permission, George. Go on. I'm staying here with the rest of the guys."

He didn't move. "You and me, Sammy, we'll stick together." He grinned and draped his arm around my shoulders.

I twisted away, and walked across the prison yard. All we had in common was red hair. He worried me: I couldn't figure out what his angle was on suddenly becoming a great pal of mine. And George was the kind of guy who always had an angle.

He followed me across the yard, and put his big arm around my shoulders again. "O.K., Sammy, we'll stay here and wait."

"I don't give a damn what you do."

"O.K., O.K.," he laughed. "I was just going to suggest, since we got an hour or so to wait, why don't you and me go down the road a piece and see if we can't get us some smokes and souvenirs? Both speaking German, we ought to make out real good, you and me."

I was dying for a smoke, and he knew it. I'd traded him my gloves for two cigarettes a couple of months before—when it had been plenty cold—and I hadn't had one since. George started me thinking about what that first inhale would be like. There'd be cigarettes in the nearest town, Peterswald, two uphill miles away.

"Whaddya say, Sammy?"

I shrugged. "What the hell—let's go."

"Attaboy."

"Where you going?" yelled one of the guys in the prison yard.

"Out to have us a quick look around," George answered.

"Be back in an hour," I added.

"Want some company?" yelled the guy.

George kept on walking, and didn't answer. "Get a mob, and they'll louse up everything," he said winking. "Two's just right."

I looked at him. He had a smile fixed on his face, but that didn't keep me from seeing that he was still plenty scared.

"What are you afraid of, George?"

"Old Georgie afraid of something? That'll be the day."

We took our place in the noisy crowd, and began to climb the gentle grade to Peterswald.

II.

Sometimes, when I think about what happened in Peterswald, I make excuses for myself—that I was drunk, that I was a little crazy after having been locked up and hungry for so long. The hell of it is that I wasn't forced into doing what I did. I wasn't cornered. I did it because I wanted to.

Peterswald wasn't what I'd expected. I'd hoped for at least a store or two where we could beg or steal a couple of cigarettes and something to eat. But the town wasn't anything more than two dozen farms, each with a wall and a ten-foot gate. They were jammed together on a green hilltop, overlooking the fields, so that they formed a solid fort. With tanks and artillery on their way, though, Peterswald was nothing but a pretty push-over, and it didn't look like anybody felt like making the Russians fight for it.

Here and there a white flag—a bedsheet on the end of a broomstick—fluttered from a second-story window. Every gate stood open—unconditional surrender.

"This looks as good as any," said George. He gripped my arm, steered me out of the mob, through the gate, and into the hard-packed courtyard of the first farm we came to.

The yard was closed in on three sides by the house and farm buildings, with the wall and gate across the fourth. Looking through the open doors into the vacant barns, and through the windows into the still house, I felt for the first time like what I really was—a worried stranger. Up to then, I'd walked, talked, and acted as though I was a special case, an American, somehow out of this European mess, without a damn thing to be afraid of. Walking into a ghost town changed my mind—

Or maybe I was beginning to be afraid of George. Saying that now may be hindsight—I don't know for sure.

Maybe, down deep, I *was* starting to wonder. His eyes were too big and interested whenever I said something, and he couldn't keep his hands off me, pawing, patting, slapping; and every time he talked about what he wanted to do next, it was "You and me, Sammy . . ."

"Hello!" he shouted. He got a quick echo from the walls around us, and then silence. He still held my arm, and he gave it a squeeze. "Ain't this cozy, Sammy? Looks like we got the place all to ourselves." He pushed the big gate shut, and slid the thick wooden cross-bar across it. I don't think I could have budged the gate then, but George had moved it without even changing his expression. He walked back to my side, dusting his hands and grinning.

"What's the angle, George?"

"To the victor go the spoils—ain't that right?" He kicked open the front door. "Well, go on in, kid. Help yourself. Georgie's just fixed things so nobody's going to bother us till we've got the pick of the stuff. Go find something real nice for your mother and your girlfriend, huh?"

"All I want is a smoke," I said. "You can open the damn gate as far as I'm concerned."

George took a package of cigarettes from his field jacket pocket. "Here's the kind of buddy I am," he laughed. "Have one."

"What's the idea of making me walk all the way to Peterswald for a cigarette, when you had a whole pack?"

He walked into the house. "I like your company, Sammy. You ought to feel real complimented. Redheads ought to stick together."

"Let's get out of here, George."

"The gate's shut. There's nothing to be afraid of, Sammy, just like you said. Brighten up. Go out in the kitchen and get something to eat. That's all that's the matter with you. You'll kick yourself for the rest of your life if you pass up a deal like this." He turned his back, and started pulling out drawers, emptying them on a tabletop, and picking over the contents. He whistled an old dance tune I hadn't heard since the late thirties.

I stood in the middle of the room, getting a dizzy, dreamy lift out of the first deep drags on the cigarette. I closed my eyes, and, when I opened them again, George didn't worry me anymore. There wasn't anything to be afraid of—the growing nightmare feeling was gone. I relaxed.

"Whoever lived here took off in a hurry," said George, still with his back to me. He held up a small bottle. "Forgot their heart medicine. My old lady used to have this stuff around the house for her heart." He laid it back in the drawer. "Same in German as it is in English. Funny thing about strychnine, Sammy—little doses can save your life." He dropped a pair of earrings into his bulging pocket. "These'll make some little girl very happy," he said.

"If she likes stuff from the five-and-ten, they will."

"Cheer up, will you, Sammy? What're you trying to do, spoil your buddy's good time? Go out in the kitchen and get yourself something to eat, for God's sake. I'll be along in a minute."

As far as being a victor and getting some spoils goes, I didn't do badly in my own way—three slices of black bread and a wedge of cheese, waiting for me on the kitchen table in the back of the house. I looked in a cabinet drawer for a knife to cut the cheese with, and got a little surprise. There was a knife, all right, but there was also a pistol, not much bigger than my fist, and a full clip beside it. I played with it, figured out how it worked, and shoved the clip into place to see if it really belonged with the gun. It was a pretty thing— a nice souvenir. I shrugged, and started to put it back. It'd be suicide to be caught with a gun by the Russians today.

"Sammy! Where the hell are you?" called George.

I slipped the gun into my trouser pocket. "Here in the kitchen, George. What did you find—the crown jewels?"

"Better'n that, Sammy." His face was a bright pink, and he was breathing hard when he came into the room. He looked fatter than he really was, with his field jacket jammed full of junk he'd picked up in the other rooms. He banged a bottle of brandy on the table. "How you like the looks of that, Sammy? Now you and me can have ourselves a little victory party, huh? Now don't go home to Jersey and tell your folks old Georgie never gave you nothing." He slapped my back. "She was full when I found her, and she's half gone now, Sammy—so you're way behind the party."

"I'll stay that way, George. Thanks, but it'd probably kill me, the shape I'm in."

He sat down in the chair facing me, with a big, loose grin on his face. "Finish your sandwich, and you'll be ready for one. The war's over, boy! Is that something to drink to, or is it?"

"Later maybe."

He didn't take another drink himself. He sat quietly for a while, thinking hard about something, and I munched my food in silence.

"What's the matter with your appetite?" I asked at last.

"Nothing. Good as ever. I ate this morning."

"Thanks for offering me some. What was it, a farewell gift from the guards?"

He smiled, as though I'd just paid tribute to him for the slick deals he'd pulled. "What's the matter, Sammy—hate my guts or something?"

"Did I say anything?"

"You don't have to, kid. You're like all the rest." He leaned back in his chair and stretched his arms. "I hear some of the boys are going to turn me in as a collaborator when we get back to the States. You going to do that, Sammy?" He was perfectly calm, yawning. He went right on, without giving me a chance to answer. "Poor old

Georgie hasn't got a friend in the world, has he? He's really on his own now, ain't he? I guess the rest of you boys'll be flown right home, but I imagine the Army will want to have a little talk with Georgie Fisher, won't they, huh?"

"You're boiled, George. Forget it. Nobody's going to—"

He stood up, steadying himself with a hand on the table. "Nope, Sammy, I got it doped out just right. Being a collaborator—that's treason, ain't it? They can hang you for that, can't they?"

"Take it easy, George. Nobody's going to try and hang you." I stood up slowly.

"I said I got it doped out just right, Sammy. Georgie Fisher's no man to be, so what do you think I'm gonna do?" He fumbled with his shirt collar, pulled out his dogtags, and threw them on the floor. "I'm gonna be somebody else, Sammy. I'd say that was real bright, wouldn't you?"

The noise of the tanks was beginning to make the dishes in the cupboard hum. I started for the door. "I don't give a damn what you do, George. I won't turn you in. All I want is to get home in one piece, and I'm heading back for camp right now."

George stepped between me and the door, and rested his hand on my shoulder. He winked and grinned. "Wait a minute, kid. You ain't heard it all, yet. Don't you want to hear what your buddy Georgie's going to do next? You'll be real interested."

"So long, George."

He didn't get out of my way. "Better sit down and have a drink, Sammy. Calm your nerves. You and me, kid, neither one of us is going back to camp. The boys back there know what Georgie Fisher looks like, and that'd spoil everything, wouldn't it? Think I'd be smart to wait a couple of days, then turn myself in down at Prague, where nobody knows me."

"I said I wouldn't say anything, George, and I won't."

"I said sit down, Sammy. Have a drink."

I was woozy and weary, and the tough black bread in my stomach was making me feel sick. I sat.

"That's my buddy," he said. "This won't take long, if you see things my way, Sammy. I said I was going to quit being Georgie Fisher and be somebody else."

"Good, fine, George."

"The thing is, I'll need a new name and dogtags to go with it. I like yours—what'll you take for 'em?" He stopped smiling. He wasn't fooling—he was making me a deal. He leaned over the table, and, with his fat, pink, sweaty face a few inches from mine, he whispered, "Whaddya say, Sammy? Two hundred bucks cash and this watch for the tags. That'd damn near pay for a new LaSalle, wouldn't it? Look at the watch, Sammy—worth a thousand bucks in New York—strikes the hours, tells you what the date is—"

Funny, George forgetting LaSalle was out of business. He pulled a roll of bills from his hip pocket. The Germans had taken our money from us when we'd been captured, but some of the boys had hidden bills in the lining of their clothes. George, with his corner on cigarettes, had managed to get just about every cent the Germans had missed. Supply and demand—five bucks a smoke.

But the watch was a surprise. George had kept it a secret up to now—for very good reasons. The watch had belonged to Jerry Sullivan, the kid who'd been shot in the prison break.

"Where'd you get Jerry's watch, George?"

George shrugged. "A beauty, ain't it? Gave Jerry a hundred smokes for it. Cleaned me out to do it."

"When, George?"

He wasn't giving me his big, confidential grin anymore. He was mean and surly. "Whaddya mean, *when*? Just before he got it, if you want to know." He ran his hands through his hair. "O.K., go ahead and say I got him killed. That's what you're thinking, so go ahead and say it."

"I wasn't thinking that, George. I was just thinking how lucky you were to put that deal over. Jerry told me the watch had been his grandfather's, and he wouldn't take anything for it. That's all. I was just kind of surprised he made the deal," I said softly.

"What's the use?" he said angrily. "How can I prove I didn't have anything to do with that? You guys pinned that on me because I had it good and you didn't. I played square with Jerry, and I'll kill the guy who says I didn't. And now

I'm playing square with you, Sammy. Do you want the dough and the watch or not?"

I was thinking back to the night of the break, remembering what Jerry had said just before he started crawling into the tunnel. "God, I wish I had a cigarette," he'd said.

The noise of the tanks was almost a roar now. They must be past the camp, climbing the last mile to Peterswald, I thought. Not much more time to play for. "Sure, George, it's a good deal. Swell, but what am I supposed to do while you're me?"

"Almost nothing, kid. All you do is forget who you are for a while. Turn yourself in at Prague, and tell 'em you've lost your memory. Stall 'em just long enough for me to get back to the States. Ten days, Sammy—that's all. It'll work, kid, with both of us redheads and the same height."

"So what happens when they find out *I'm* Sam Kleinhans?"

"I'll be over the hill in the States. They'll never find me." He was getting impatient. "C'mon, Sammy, is it a deal?"

It was a crack-brained scheme, without a prayer of working. I looked into George's eyes, and thought I saw that he knew that, too. Maybe, with a buzz on, he thought it would work—but now he seemed to be changing his mind. I looked at the watch on the table, and thought of Jerry Sullivan being carried back into camp dead. George had helped carry him, I remembered.

I thought of the gun in my pocket. "Go to hell, George," I said.

He didn't look surprised. He pushed the bottle in front of me. "Have a drink and think it over," he said evenly. "You're just making things tough for both of us." I pushed the bottle back. "Very tough," said George. "I want the tags awful bad, Sammy."

I braced myself, but nothing happened. He was a bigger coward than I thought.

George held out the watch, and pushed down the winder with his thumb. "Listen, Sammy—it strikes the hours."

I didn't hear the chimes. All hell cut loose outside—the deafening clank and thunder of tanks, backfiring, and wild, happy singing, with accordions screaming above it all.

"They're here!" I yelled. The war really was over! I could believe it now. I forgot George, Jerry, the watch—everything but the wonderful noise. I ran to the window. Big puffs of smoke and dust billowed up over the wall, and there was a banging on the gate. "This is it!" I laughed.

George yanked me back from the window, and pushed me against the wall. "This is it, all right!" he said. His face was filled with terror. He held a pistol against my chest. George clawed at my dogtag chain, snapped it with a quick jerk.

There was a sharp, splintering noise, a metallic groan, and the gate sprung open. A tank stood in the opening, racing its engine, its huge treads resting against the shattered gate. George turned to face the noise, just as two Russian soldiers slid from roosts atop the tank turret, and trotted into the courtyard, their submachine guns leveled. They looked quickly from window to window, and yelled something I couldn't understand.

"They'll kill us if they see that gun!" I cried.

George nodded. He seemed to be stunned, in a dream. "Yeah," he said, and he threw the gun across the room. It slithered along the bleached floorboards, coming to rest in a dark corner. "Put your hands up, Sammy," he said. He held his hands over his head, his back to me, facing the hallway down which the Russians were stomping. "I must of been crazy drunk, Sammy. I was out of my head," he whispered.

"Sure, George—sure you were."

"We got to stick together through this, Sammy, you hear?"

"Stick through what?" I kept my hands at my sides. "Hey Rooskie, how the hell are you?" I shouted.

The two Russians, rough-looking teen-agers, strutted into the room, their submachine guns ready. Neither one smiled. "Put your hands up!" commanded one in German.

"Amerikaner," I said weakly, and I put my hands up.

The two looked surprised, and began consulting in whispers, never taking their eyes off us. They scowled at first, but became more and more jovial as they talked, until they were at last beaming at us. I guess they had had to reassure each other that it was right in line with policy to be friendly with Americans.

"It's a great day for the people," said the one who could speak German, gravely.

"A great day," I agreed. "George, give the boys a drink."

They looked happily at the bottle, and rocked back and forth on their feet, nodding and snickering. They insisted politely that George take the first drink to the great day for the people. George grinned nervously. The bottle was almost to his lips before it slipped from his fingers to bang on the floor, spewing its contents over our feet.

"God, I'm sorry," said George.

I leaned over to pick it up, but the Russians stopped me. "Vodka is better than that German poison," said the German-speaking Russian solemnly, and he drew a large bottle from his blouse. "Roosevelt!" he said, taking a big gulp, and passing the bottle to George.

The bottle went around four times: in honor of Roosevelt, Stalin, Churchill, and of Hitler's roasting in hell. The last toast was my idea. "Over a slow fire," I added. The Russians thought that was pretty rich, but their laughter died instantly when an officer appeared at the gate to bellow for them. They gave us quick salutes, snatched the bottle, and rushed out of the house.

We watched them climb aboard the tank, which backed

away from the gate and lumbered down the road. The two of them waved.

The vodka had made me feel fuzzy, hot, and wonderful— and, it turned out, cocky and bloodthirsty. George was almost blind drunk, swaying.

"I didn't know what I was doing, Sammy. I was—" The sentence trailed off. He was making for the corner where his gun lay—surly, weaving, squinting.

I stepped in front of him, and pulled the tiny pistol from my trouser pocket. "Look what I found, Georgie."

He stopped and blinked at it. "Looks like a nice one, Sammy." He held out his hand. "Let's have a look at it."

I snapped off the safety catch. "Sit down, Georgie, old friend."

He sank into the chair where I had sat at the table. "I don't get it," he mumbled. "You wouldn't shoot your old buddy, would you, Sammy?" He looked at me pleadingly. "I offered you a square deal, didn't I? Ain't I always been—"

"You're too bright to think I'd let you get away with this dogtag deal, aren't you? I'm no buddy of yours, and you know it, don't you, Georgie? The only way it'd work would be with me dead. Didn't you figure it that way, too?"

"Everybody's down on old George, ever since Jerry got it. I swear to God, Sammy, I never had anything to do with—" He didn't finish the sentence. George shook his head and sighed.

"Pretty tough about poor old Georgie—not even enough guts to shoot me when you had the chance." I picked up the bottle George had dropped and set it in front of him. "What you need is a good drink. See, George?—three good shots left. Aren't you glad it didn't all spill?"

"Don't want no more, Sammy." He closed his eyes. "Put away that gun, will you? I never meant you no harm."

"I said take a drink." He didn't move. I sat down opposite him, still covering him with the gun. "Give me the watch, George."

He seemed to wake up all of a sudden. "Is that what you're after? Sure, Sammy, here it is, if that'll make things square. How can I explain how I get when I'm drunk? I just lose control of myself, kid." He handed me Jerry's watch. "Here, Sammy. After all old Georgie's put you through, God knows you've earned it."

I set the watch hands at noon, and pushed down the winder. The tiny chimes sounded twelve times, striking twice each second.

"Worth a thousand bucks in New York, Sammy," said George thickly, as the chimes rang.

"That's how long you have to drink out of that bottle, George," I said, "as long as it takes the watch to strike twelve."

"I don't get it. What's the big idea?"

I laid the watch on the table. "Like you said, George, it's a funny thing about strychnine—a little of it can save your life." I pushed the winder on the watch again. "Have a drink to Jerry Sullivan, buddy."

The chimes tinkled again. Eight . . . nine . . . ten . . . eleven . . . twelve. The room was quiet.

"O.K., so I didn't drink," said George, grinning. "So what happens now, Boy Scout?"

III.

When I began this story, I said I thought it was a murder story. I'm not sure.

I made it back to the American lines, all right, and I reported that George had killed himself accidentally with a pistol he'd found in a ditch. I signed an affidavit swearing it had happened that way.

What the hell, he was dead, and that was that, wasn't it? Who'd have benefited if I'd told them I shot George? My soul? George's soul, maybe?

Well, Army Intelligence smelled something fishy about the story quick enough. At Camp Lucky Strike, near Le Havre, France, where they had all of the repatriated prisoners of war waiting for boats home, I got called into a tent Intelligence had set up there. I'd been in camp for two weeks, and was due to ship out the next afternoon.

A gray-haired major asked the questions. He had the affidavit in front of him, and he passed over the story about the pistol in the ditch without showing much interest. He quizzed me for quite a while about how George had behaved in prison camp, and he wanted to know exactly what George looked like. He took notes on what I told him.

"Sure you have the name right?" he asked.

"Yessir, and the serial number, too. Here's one of his dogtags, sir. I left the other one with the body. Sorry, sir, I meant to turn this in before now."

The major studied the tag, finally fastened it to the affidavit, and slipped both into a thick folder. I could see George's name written on the outside. "I don't know exactly what to do with this next," he said, toying with the tie-string on the folder. "Quite a guy, George Fisher." He offered me a cigarette. I took it, but I didn't light it right away.

This was it. God knows how, but they'd found out the whole story, I thought. I wanted to yell, but I kept on smiling, my teeth clamped together hard.

The major took his time about phrasing the next sentence. "The tag is a phony," he said at last, smiling a little. "There's nobody by that name missing from the U.S. Army." He leaned forward to light my cigarette. "Maybe we'd better turn this folder over to the Germans so they can notify the next of kin."

I'd never seen George Fisher before they brought him into prison camp alone that day eight months previous, but I should have known the type. I grew up with a couple of kids like him. He must have been a good Nazi to get his job in German Intelligence, because as I said, most of the *Bund* kids didn't do that well. I don't know how many of them got back to the U.S. when the war ended, but my buddy George Fisher damn near made it.

The Commandant's Desk

I was sitting before the window of my small cabinet-making shop in the Czechoslovakian town of Beda. My widowed daughter, Marta, held the curtain back for me, and watched the Americans through one corner of the window, being careful not to block any of my view with her head.

"I wish he would turn this way, so we could see his face," I said impatiently. "Marta, pull the curtain back more."

"Is he a general?" said Marta.

"A general as commandant for Beda?" I laughed. "A corporal, maybe. How well fed they all look, eh? Aaaaaah, they eat—*how* they eat!" I ran my hand along the back of my black cat. "Now, kitty, you have only to cross the street for your first taste of American cream." I raised my hands over my head. "Marta! Do you feel it, do you *feel* it? The Russians are gone, Marta, they're gone!"

And now, we were trying to see the face of the American commandant, who was moving into the building across the street—where the Russian commandant had been a few weeks before. The Americans went inside, kicking their way through rubbish and splintered furniture. For a while, there was nothing to see through my window. I leaned back in my chair and closed my eyes.

"It's over, the killing is all over," I said, "and we're alive. Did you think that was possible? Did anyone in his right mind expect to be alive when it was over?"

"I feel almost as though being alive were something to be ashamed of," she said.

"The world will probably feel that way for a long, long time. You can at least thank God you've come through it all with very little guilt in all the killing. Having been helpless in the middle has that advantage. Think of the guilt on the shoulders of the Americans—a hundred thousand dead in the Moscow bombings, fifty thousand in Kiev—"

"What about the guilt of the Russians?" she said passionately.

"No—not the Russians. That's one of the joys of losing a war. You surrender your guilt along with your capital, and join the ranks of the innocent little people."

The cat rubbed her flanks against my wooden leg and purred. I suppose most men with wooden legs conceal the fact as best they can. I lost my left leg as an Austrian infantryman in 1916, and I wear one trouser leg higher than the other to show off the handsome oak peg I made for myself after World War I. Carved in the peg are the images of Georges Clemenceau, David Lloyd George, and Woodrow Wilson, who helped the Czech Republic rise from the ruins of the Austro-Hungarian Empire in 1919, when I was twenty-five. And below these images are two more, each within a wreath: Tomáš Masaryk and Eduard Beneš, the first leaders of the Republic. There are other faces that should be added, and now, now that peace is with us once again, perhaps I'll carve them. The only carving I've done on the peg in the past thirty years is crude and obscure, and maybe barbaric—three deep nicks near the iron tip, for the three German officers whose car I sent down a mountainside one night in 1943, during the Nazi occupation.

These men across the street weren't the first Americans I'd seen. I owned a furniture factory in Prague during the days of the Republic, and I did a great deal of business with buyers for American department stores. When the Nazis came, I lost my factory, and moved to Beda, this quiet town in the foothills of Sudetenland. My wife died soon after that, of the rarest of causes, the natural ones. Then I had only my daughter, Marta.

Now, praise God, I was seeing Americans again—after the Nazis, after the Russian Army of World War II, after the Czech communists, after the Russians again. Knowing this day was coming had kept me alive. Hidden under the floorboards of my workshop was a bottle of Scotch that had constantly tried my willpower. But I left it in its hiding-place. It was to be my present to the Americans when they finally came.

"They're coming out," said Marta.

I opened my eyes to see a stocky, red-headed American major staring at me from across the street, his hands on his hips. He looked tired and annoyed. Another young man, a captain, tall, massive, and slow, and very Italian-looking except for his stature, strode out of the building to join him.

Stupidly, perhaps, I blinked back at them. "They're coming over here!" I said excitedly, helplessly.

The major and the captain walked in, each looking down at a blue pamphlet, which I gathered contained Czech phrases. The big captain seemed self-conscious, and I sensed that the red-headed major was a little belligerent.

The captain ran his finger down the margin of a page, and shook his head dispiritedly. "'Machine gun, mortar, motorcycle . . . tank, tourniquet, trench.' Nothing about filing cabinets, desks, or chairs."

"What the hell you expect?" said the major. "It's a book for soldiers, not a bunch of pansy clerks." He scowled at the pamphlet, said something completely unintelligible, and looked up at me expectantly. "There's one hell of a swell book," he said. "Says that's the way to ask for an interpreter, and the old man acts like it was Ubangi poetry."

"Gentlemen, I speak English," I said, "and my daughter, Marta, too."

"By God, he really does," said the major. "Good for you, Pop." He made me feel like a small dog, who had cleverly—for a small dog—fetched him a rubber ball.

I held out my hand to the major, and told him my name. He looked down at my hand superciliously, and kept his hands in his pockets. I felt myself reddening.

"My name is Captain Paul Donnini," said the other man quickly, "and this is Major Lawson Evans." He shook my hand. "Sir," he said to me—his voice was paternal and deep—"the Russians—"

The major used an epithet that made my jaw drop, and amazed Marta, who has heard soldiers talk for the better part of her life.

Captain Donnini was embarrassed. "They haven't left a stick of furniture," he continued, "and I'm wondering if you could let us have some of the pieces in your shop here."

"I was going to offer you them," I said. "It's a tragedy they smashed everything. They confiscated the most beautiful furniture in Beda." I smiled and shook my head. "Aaaaah, those enemies of capitalists—they had their quarters fixed up like a little Versailles."

"We saw the wreckage," said the captain.

"And then, when they couldn't have the treasures anymore, then no one could have them." I made a motion like a man swinging an axe. "And the world becomes a little duller for us all—for there being fewer treasures. Bourgeois treasures, maybe, but those who can't afford beautiful things love the idea of there being such things somewhere."

The captain nodded pleasantly, but, to my surprise, I saw that my words had somehow irritated Major Evans.

"Well, anyway," I said, "I want you to take whatever you need. It will be an honor to help you." I was wondering if now was the opportune time to offer the Scotch. Things weren't going quite as I'd expected.

"He's real smart, Pop is," said the major acidly.

I suddenly realized what it was the major had been implying. It was a shock. He was telling me that I was one of the enemy. He meant that I should cooperate because I was afraid; he wanted me to be afraid.

For an instant, I was physically sick. Once, as a much younger and more Christian man, I liked to say that men who depended on fear to get things done were sick and pathetic and pitifully alone. Later, after having seen whole armies of such men in action, I saw that I was the kind that was alone—and maybe sick and pathetic, too, but I would have killed myself rather than admit that.

I had to be wrong about the new commandant. I told myself I'd been suspicious and—now that I'm old, I can say it—afraid too long. But Marta felt the threat, the fear in the air, too, I could tell. She was hiding her warmth, as she had hidden it for years, behind a dull, prim mask.

"Yes," I said, "you are welcome to anything you can use." The major pushed open the door of the back room, where I sleep and do my work. I was through being host. I sank back down in my chair by the window. Captain Donnini, ill at ease, stayed with Marta and me.

"It's very beautiful here in the mountains," he said lamely.

We lapsed into an uncomfortable silence, broken from time to time by the major's rummaging about in the back room. I took a good look at the captain, and was struck by how much more boyish he seemed than the major, though it was quite possible that they were the same age. It was hard to imagine him on a battlefield, and it was hard to imagine the major anywhere else.

I heard Major Evans give a low whistle, and I knew he'd found the commandant's desk.

"The major must have been a very brave man, he has so many medals," said Marta at last.

Captain Donnini seemed grateful for a chance to explain about his superior. "He was and is an extremely brave man," he said warmly. He said that the major and most of the enlisted men in Beda had come from an apparently famous armored division, which, the captain implied, never knew fear or fatigue, and loved nothing better than a good fight.

I clucked my tongue in wonderment, as I always do when hearing of such a division. I have heard of them from

American officers, German officers, Russian officers; and my officers in World War I solemnly declared that I belonged to such a division. When I hear of a division of war-lovers from an enlisted man, maybe I will believe it, provided the man is sober and has been shot at. If there are such divisions, perhaps they should be preserved between wars in dry ice.

"And what about you?" said Marta, breaking into the captain's blood-and-thunder biography of Major Evans.

He smiled. "I'm so new to Europe, I can't—if you'll pardon the expression—find my behind with both hands. The air of Fort Benning, Georgia, is still in my lungs. The major—he's the hero, been fighting for three years without a break."

"And I didn't figure to wind up here as a combination constable, county clerk, and wailing wall," said Major Evans, standing in the doorway of the back room. "Pop, I want this desk. Making it for yourself, were you?"

"What would I do with a desk like that? I was building it for the Russian commandant."

"A friend of yours, eh?"

I tried to smile, unconvincingly, I imagine. "I wouldn't be here to talk to you, if I'd refused to make it. And I wouldn't have been here to talk to *him*, if I hadn't made a bed for the Nazi commandant—with a garland of swastikas and the first stanza of the Horst Wessel Song on the headboard."

The captain smiled with me, but the major didn't. "*This* one is different," said the major. "*He* comes right out and says he was a collaborator."

"I didn't say that," I said evenly.

"Don't spoil it, don't spoil it," said Major Evans, "it's a refreshing change."

Marta suddenly hurried upstairs.

"I was no collaborator," I said.

"Sure, sure—fought 'em every inch of the way. You bet. I know, I know. Come here a minute, will you? I want to talk about my desk."

He was seated on the unfinished desk, an enormous and, to me, hideous piece of furniture. I'd designed it as a private satire on the Russian commandant's bad taste and hypocrisy about symbols of wealth. I'd made it as ornate and pretentious as possible, a Russian peasant's dream of what a Wall Street banker's desk looked like. It glittered with bits of colored glass set like jewels in the wood, and it was highlighted with radiator paint that looked something like gilt. Now it appeared that the satire would have to remain private, for the American commandant was as taken by it as the Russian had been.

"This is what I call a piece of furniture," said Major Evans.

"Very nice," said Captain Donnini absently. He was looking up the stairs, where Marta had fled.

"There's just one thing wrong with it, Pop."

"The hammer and sickle—I know. I was going to take—"

"How right you are," said the major. He drew back his boot, and gave the massive escutcheon a savage kick on its edge. The round piece broke free, rolled drunkenly into a corner, and settled face down with a rowrroworrowrr—clack! The cat investigated it, and backed away suspiciously.

"An eagle goes there, Pop." The major took off his cap to show me the American eagle on it. "Like this one."

"Not a simple design. It'll take a while," I said.

"Not as simple as a swastika or a hammer and sickle, eh?"

I'd dreamed for weeks of sharing the joke of the desk with the Americans, of telling them about the secret drawer I'd built in for the Russian commandant, the richest joke of all. Now, the Americans were here; and I felt little different than before—rotten and lost and lonely. I didn't feel like sharing anything with anyone but Marta.

"No," I said, answering the major's poisonous question. "No, sir." What was I supposed to say?

The Scotch stayed under the floorboards, and the secret drawer in the desk remained a secret.

The American garrison in Beda was about a hundred men, almost all of them, save Captain Donnini, veterans of years of fighting in the same armored division from which Major Evans had come. They behaved like conquerors, with Major Evans encouraging them to do just that. I'd expected a great deal of the coming of the Americans—a rebirth of pride and dignity for Marta and me; a little prosperity and good things to eat, too; and for Marta, the better part of a lifetime worth living. Instead, there was the bullying distrust of Major Evans, the new commandant, multiplied a hundred times in the persons of his men.

In the nightmare of a warring world, it takes peculiar skills to get along. One of these is the understanding of the psychology of occupation troops. The Russians weren't like the Nazis, and the Americans were very different from either. There wasn't the physical violence of the Russians and Nazis, thank God—no shootings or torture. What was particularly interesting was that the Americans had to get drunk before they could make real trouble. Unfortunately for Beda, Major Evans let them get drunk as often as they liked. When they were drunk, they were fond of stealing— in the name of souvenir hunting—driving jeeps through the street at breakneck speeds, firing guns in the air, shouting obscenities, picking fistfights, and breaking windows.

The people of Beda were so used to keeping silent and out of sight, no matter what happened, that it took us a while to discover the really basic difference between the Americans and the others. The Americans' toughness, callousness, was very shallow, and beneath it was grave misgiving. We discovered that they could be embarrassed easily by women or older men who would stand up to them like parents, and scold them for what they were doing. This sobered most of them up as quickly as buckets of cold water would have.

With that insight into our conquerors, we were able to make things a little more bearable, but not much. There was the crushing realization that we were regarded as the enemy, little different from the Russians, and that the major wanted us punished. The townspeople were organized into labor battalions, and put to work under armed guard, like prisoners of war. What made the labor particularly deadly is that it wasn't concerned with repairing the war damage to the town so much as with making the American garrison's quarters more comfortable, and with building a huge and ugly monument honoring the Americans who had died in the battle for Beda. Four had died. Major Evans made the atmosphere of the town the atmosphere of a prison. Shame was the order of the day, and budding pride or hope was promptly nipped. We weren't entitled to them.

There was one bright spot—an American unhappier than any of us—Captain Donnini. It was up to him to carry out the major's orders, and getting drunk, which he tried several times, didn't do for him what it did for the others. He carried out the orders with a reluctance I'm sure he could have been court-martialed for. Moreover, he spent as much time with Marta and me as he did with the major, and most of his talk with us was a guarded apology for what he had to do. Curiously, Marta and I found ourselves comforting this sad, dark giant, rather than the other way around.

I thought about the major as I stood at my workbench in the back room, finishing up the American eagle for the front of the new commandant's desk. Marta lay on my cot, staring at the ceiling. Her shoes were white with rock dust. She had been working all day on the monument.

"Well," I said gloomily, "if I'd been fighting for three years, I wonder how friendly I would be. Let's face it, whether all of us wanted to or not, we gave men and materials that helped to kill hundreds of thousands of Americans." I gestured at the mountains to the west. "Look where the Russians got their uranium."

"Eye for eye, tooth for tooth," said Marta. "How long does that go on?"

I sighed and shook my head. "The Czechs have paid with interest, God knows. Hand for hand, foot for foot, burning for burning, wound for wound, stripe for stripe." We'd lost most of our young men, Marta's husband among them, in suicide waves before main Russian attacks; and our largest cities were little more than gravel and smoke.

"And, after paying it, we get a new commissar. They're no different from the rest," she said bitterly. "It was childish to expect anything else."

Her terrible disappointment, for which I'd built her up, her apathy and hopelessness—good God in Heaven, I couldn't bear it! And there would be no more liberators. The only strength left anywhere in the world was in America, and the Americans were in Beda.

Dully, I set to work on the American eagle again. The captain had given me a dollar bill from which to copy the insignia. "Let me see—nine, ten, eleven, twelve, thirteen arrows in the claw."

There was a diffident knock on the door, and Captain Donnini walked in. "Pardon me," he said.

"I guess we'll have to," I said. "Your side won the war."

"Afraid I didn't have much to do with it."

"The major didn't leave anybody for the captain to shoot," said Marta.

"What happened to your window?" said the captain.

There was shattered glass all over the floor, and a big piece of cardboard now kept the weather from coming in the window. "It was liberated last night by a beer bottle," I said. "I've written the major a note about it—for which I'll probably be beheaded."

"What's that you're making?"

"An eagle with thirteen arrows in one claw, and an olive branch in the other."

"You're well-off. You could be whitewashing rocks. You were kept off the list, just so you could finish the desk."

"Yes, I saw the rock whitewashers," I said. "With the whitewashed rocks, Beda looks better than it did before the war. You'd never know it had been shelled." The major had ordered that a stirring message be written on his lawn in whitewashed rock: *1402 MP Company, Major Lawson Evans Commanding.* The flower beds and walks were also being outlined in rock.

"Oh, he's not a bad man," said the captain. "It's a miracle he's come through it all as well as he has."

"It's a miracle any of us have come through as well as we have," said Marta.

"Yes, I realize that. I know—you've been through terrible times. But, well, so has the major. He lost his family in the Chicago bombings, his wife and three children."

"I lost my husband in the war," said Marta.

"So what are you trying to tell us—that we're all doing penance for the death of the major's family? Does he think we wanted them killed?" I said.

He leaned against the workbench, and closed his eyes. "Oh hell, I don't know, I don't know. I thought it would help you to understand him—make you not hate him. Nothing makes any sense, though—nothing seems to help."

"Did you think you could help, Captain?" said Marta.

"Before I came over here—yes, I did. Now I know I'm not what's needed, and I don't know what is. I sympathize with everybody, damn it, and see why they are the way they are—you two, all the people in town, the major, the enlisted men. Maybe, if I'd got a bullet through me or had somebody come after me with a flame-thrower, maybe I'd be more of a man."

"And hate like everyone else," said Marta.

"Yes—and be as sure of myself as everybody else seems to be on account of it."

"Not sure—*numb*," I said.

"Numb," he repeated, "everyone has reasons for being numb."

"That's the last defense," said Marta. "Numbness or suicide."

"Marta!" I said.

"You know it's true," she said flatly. "If gas chambers were set up on European street corners, they'd have longer queues than the bakeries. When does all the hate end? Never."

"Marta, for the love of Heaven, I won't have you talking that way," I said.

"Major Evans talks that way, too," said Captain Donnini. "Only he says he wants to go on fighting. Once or twice, when he's been tight, he's said he wished he'd been killed—that there wasn't anything to go home to. He took fantastic chances in the fighting, and never got a scratch."

"Poor man," said Marta, "no more war."

"Well, there's still guerrilla action—a lot of it around Leningrad. He's applied for a transfer there, so he can get into it." He looked down and spread his fingers over his knees. "Well, anyway, what I came to tell you was that the major wants his desk tomorrow."

The door swung open, and the major strode into the workshop. "Captain, where the hell have you been? I sent you on an errand that should have taken five minutes, and you've been gone thirty."

Captain Donnini stood at attention. "Sorry, sir."

"You know how I feel about my men fraternizing with the enemy."

"Yessir."

He confronted me. "Now what's this about your window?"

"One of your men broke it last night."

"Now, isn't that too damn bad?" It was another one of his unanswerable questions. "I said, isn't that too damn bad, Pop?"

"Yes, sir."

"Pop, I'm going to tell you something that I want you to get through your head. And then I want you to make sure everybody else in town understands it."

"Yes, sir."

"You've lost a war. Have you got that? And I'm not here to have you or anybody else cry on my shoulder. I'm here to see that everybody damn well understands they lost a war, and to see that nobody makes trouble. And that's all I'm here for. And the next person who tells me he was a pal of the Russians because he had to be gets his teeth kicked in. And that goes for the next person who tells me he's got it rough. You haven't got it half rough enough."

"Yes, sir."

"It's your Europe," said Marta quietly.

He turned to her angrily. "If it were mine, young lady, I'd have the engineers bulldoze the whole lousy mess flat. Nothing in it but gutless wonders who'll follow any damn dictator that comes along." Again I was struck, as I'd been on the first day, by how awfully tired and distracted he seemed.

"Sir—" said the captain.

"Be quiet. I didn't fight my way here so the Eagle Scouts could take over. Now, where's my desk?"

"I'm finishing the eagle."

"Let's have a look." I handed him the disk. He swore softly, and touched the insignia on his cap. "Like this one," he said. "I want it exactly like this one."

I blinked at the insignia on his cap. "But it is like that one. I copied exactly from a dollar bill."

"The arrows, Pop! Which claw are the arrows in?"

"Oh—on your hat they're in the right claw, on the bill they're in the left."

"All the difference in the world, Pop: one's the Army, the other's for civilians." He raised his knee, and snapped the carving over it. "Try again. You were so anxious to please the Russian commandant, please me!"

"Could I say something?" I said.

"No. All I want to hear from you is that I'll get the desk tomorrow morning."

"But the carving will take days."

"Stay up all night."

"Yes, sir."

He walked out, with the captain at his heels.

"What were you going to tell him?" said Marta, with a wry smile.

"I was going to tell him that the Czechs have fought against the Europe he hates as hard and long as he has. I was going to tell him— Oh well, what's the use?"

"Go on."

"You've heard it a thousand times, Marta. It's a tiresome story, I suppose. I wanted to tell him how I've fought the Hapsburgs and the Nazis, and then the Czech communists, and then the Russians—fought them in my own small ways. Not once have I sided with a dictator, and I never will."

"Better get to work on the eagle. Remember, arrows in the right hand."

"Marta, you've never tasted Scotch, have you?" I dug the claws of a hammer into a crack in the floor, and pried up the board. There lay the dusty bottle of Scotch I had saved for the great day of my dreams.

It was delicious, and the two of us got quite drunk. While I worked, we relived the old days, Marta and I, and for a while it seemed almost as though her mother were alive again, and Marta was a young, pretty, and carefree girl again, and we had our home and friends in Prague again, and . . . Oh God, it was lovely for a little while.

Marta fell asleep on the cot, and I hummed to myself as I chiseled out the American eagle long into the night. It was a crude, slap-dash job, and I covered its faults with putty and the fake gilt.

A few hours before sunrise, I glued the emblem to the desk, applied clamps, and dropped off to sleep. It was ready for the new commandant, exactly, save for the emblem, as I had designed it for the Russian.

They came for the desk early the next morning, a half-dozen soldiers and the captain. The desk looked like a casket for an Oriental potentate as they carried it like pall-bearers across the street. The major met them at the door, and cried warnings whenever they threatened to bump the treasure against the doorframe. The door closed, the sentry took up his position before it again, and there was nothing more to see.

I went into my workroom, cleared the shavings from the bench, and began a letter to Major Lawson Evans, 1402 MP Company, Beda, Czechoslovakia.

Dear sir: I wrote, *There is one thing about the desk I neglected to tell you. If you will look just below the eagle, you will find . . .*

I didn't take it across the street right away, although I'd intended to. It made me feel a little sick to read it over— something I never would have felt had it been addressed to the Russian commandant, who was to have received it originally. Thinking about the letter spoiled my lunch, though I haven't had enough to eat for years. Marta was too lost in her own depression to notice, though she scolds me when I don't look out for myself. She took away my untouched plate without a word.

Late in the afternoon, I drank the last of the Scotch, and walked across the street. I handed the envelope to the sentry.

"This another one about the window, Pop?" said the sentry. Apparently the window episode was a joke in wide circulation.

"No, another matter—about the desk."

"O.K., Pop."

"Thanks."

I went back to my workshop, and lay down on my cot to wait. I even managed to nap a little.

It was Marta who awakened me.

"All right, I'm ready," I murmured.

"Ready for what?"

"The soldiers."

"Not the soldiers—the major. He's leaving."

"He's what?" I threw my legs over the side of the cot.

"He's getting into a jeep with all of his equipment. Major Evans is leaving Beda!"

I hurried to the front window, and pulled aside the cardboard. Major Evans was seated in the rear of a jeep, in the midst of duffel bags, a bed roll, and other equipment. One would have thought from his appearance that a battle was raging on the outskirts of Beda. He glowered from beneath a steel helmet, and he had a carbine beside him, and a cartridge belt, knife, and pistol about his waist.

"He got his transfer," I said in wonderment.

"He's going to fight the guerrillas," laughed Marta.

"God help them."

The jeep started. Major Evans waved, and jolted away into the distance. The last I saw of the remarkable man was as the jeep reached the crest of a hill at the town's edge. He turned, thumbed his nose, and was lost from sight in the valley beyond.

Captain Donnini, across the street, caught my eye and nodded.

"Who's the new commandant?" I called.

He tapped his chest.

"What is an Eagle Scout?" whispered Marta.

"Judging from the major's tone, it's something very unsoldierly, naive, and soft-hearted. Shhhh! Here he comes."

Captain Donnini was half solemn, half amused with his new importance.

He lit a cigarette thoughtfully, and looked as though he

were trying to phrase something in his mind. "You asked when the end of hate would come," he said at last. "It comes right now. No more labor battalions, no more stealing, no more smashing. I haven't seen enough to hate." He puffed on the cigarette and thought some more. "But I'm sure I can hate the people of Beda as bitterly as Major Evans did if they don't start out tomorrow to rebuild this into a decent place for the children."

He turned quickly, and recrossed the street.

"Captain," I called, "I wrote a letter to Major Evans—"

"He turned it over to me. I haven't read it yet."

"Could I have it back?"

He looked at me questioningly. "Well, all right—it's on my desk."

"The letter is about the desk. There's something I've got to fix."

"The drawers work fine."

"There's a special drawer you don't know about."

He shrugged. "Come on."

I threw some tools into a bag, and hurried to his office. The desk sat in magnificent isolation in the middle of the otherwise spartan room. My letter lay on its top.

"You can read it, if you like," I said.

He opened the letter, and read aloud:

"Dear sir: There is one thing about the desk I neglected to tell you. If you will look just below the eagle, you will find that the oak leaf in the ornamentation can be pressed in and

turned. Turn it so that the stem points up at the eagle's left claw. Then, press down on the acorn just above the eagle, and . . ."

As he read, I followed my own directions. I pressed on the leaf and turned it, and there was a click. I pushed the acorn with my thumb, and the front of a small drawer popped out a fraction of an inch, just enough to let a person get a grip on it and pull it out the rest of the way.

"Seems to be stuck," I said. I reached up under the desk, and snipped a strand of piano wire hooked to the back of the drawer. "There!" I pulled the drawer out the rest of the way. "You see?"

Captain Donnini laughed. "Major Evans would have loved it. Wonderful!" Appreciatively, he slid the drawer back and forth several times, wondering at how its front blended so perfectly with the ornamentation. "Makes me wish I had secrets."

"There aren't many people in Europe without them," I said. He turned his back for a moment. I reached under the commandant's desk again, slipped a pin into the detonator, and removed the bomb.

Armageddon in Retrospect

Dear Friend:

May I have a minute of your time? We have never met, but I am taking the liberty of writing to you because a mutual friend has spoken of you highly as being far above average in intellect and concern for your fellow men.

The impact of each day's news being as great as it is, it is very easy for us to forget quickly major events of a few days before. Let me, then, refresh your memory on an event that shook the world five short years ago, and which is now all but forgotten, save by a few of us. I refer to what has come to be known, for good biblical reasons, as *Armageddon*.

You will remember, perhaps, the hectic beginnings at the Pine Institute. I confess that I went to work as administrator of the Institute with a sense of shame and foolishness, and for no other reason than money. I had many other offers, but the recruiter from the Institute offered to pay me twice as much as the best of them. I was in debt after three years of poverty as a graduate student, so I took the job, telling myself that I would stay one year, pay off my debts and build my savings, get a respectable job, and deny ever after that I'd been within a hundred miles of Verdigris, Oklahoma.

Thanks to this lapse in integrity, I was associated with one of the truly heroic figures of our time, Dr. Gorman Tarbell.

The assets I brought to the Pine Institute were general, chiefly the skills that go with a doctor's degree in business administration. I might as easily have applied these assets to running a tricycle factory or an amusement park. I was not in any way the creator of the theories that brought us to and through Armageddon. I arrived on the scene quite late, when much of the important thinking had been done.

Spiritually, and in terms of sacrifice, the name of Dr. Tarbell should head the list of real contributors to the campaign and victory.

Chronologically, the list should probably begin with the late Dr. Selig Schildknecht, of Dresden, Germany, who spent, by and large fruitlessly, the last half of his life and inheritance in trying to get someone to pay attention to his theories on mental illness. What Schildknecht said, in effect, was that the only unified theory of mental illness that seemed to fit all the facts was the most ancient one, which had never been disproved. He believed that the mentally ill were possessed by the Devil.

He said so in book after book, all printed at his own expense, since no publisher would touch them, and he urged that research be undertaken to find out as much as possible about the Devil, his forms, his habits, his strong points, his weaknesses.

Next on the list is an American, my former employer, Jessie L. Pine of Verdigris. Many years ago, Pine, an oil millionaire, ordered 200 feet of books for his library. The book dealer saw an opportunity to get rid of, among other gems, the collected works of Dr. Selig Schildknecht. Pine assumed that the Schildknecht volumes, since they were in a foreign language, contained passages too hot to be printed in English. So he hired the head of the University of Oklahoma's German Department to read them to him.

Far from being infuriated by the book dealer's selection, Pine was overjoyed. All his life he'd felt humiliated by his lack of education, and here he'd found a man with five university degrees whose fundamental philosophy agreed with his own, to wit: "Onliest thing in the world that's wrong with folks is that the Devil's got aholt of some of 'em."

If Schildknecht had managed to hold on to life a little longer, he wouldn't have died penniless. As it was, he missed the founding of the Jessie L. Pine Institute by only two years. From the moment of that founding on, every spurt from half the oil wells in Oklahoma was a nail in the Devil's coffin. And it was a slow day, indeed, when an opportunist of one sort or another didn't board a train for the marble halls rising in Verdigris.

The list, if I were to continue it, would get rather long, for thousands of men and women, a few of them intelligent and honest, began to explore the paths of research indicated by Schildknecht, while Pine followed doggedly with haversacks of fresh currency. But most of these men and women were jealous, incompetent passengers on one of the greatest gravy trains in history. Their experiments, usually awfully expensive, were principally satires on the ignorance and credulity of their benefactor, Jessie L. Pine.

Nothing would have come of all the millions spent, and I, for one, would have drawn my amazing paycheck without trying to deserve it, if it hadn't been for the living martyr of Armageddon, Dr. Gorman Tarbell.

He was the oldest member of the Institute, and the most reputable—about sixty, heavy, short, passionate, with long white hair, with clothes that made him look as though he spent his nights under bridges. He'd retired near Verdigris after a successful career as a physicist in a large eastern industrial research laboratory. He stopped off at the Institute one afternoon, while on his way to get groceries, to find out what on earth was going on in the impressive buildings.

I was the one who saw him first, and, perceiving him to be a man of prodigious intelligence, I did a rather sheepish job of telling him what the Institute proposed to do. My attitude conveyed that "just between the well-educated pair of us, this is a lot of hooey."

He didn't join me in my condescending smile at the project, however, but asked, instead, to see something of Dr. Schildknecht's writings. I got him the chief volume, that summarized what was said in all the others, and stood by and chuckled knowingly as he scanned it.

"Have you got any spare laboratories?" he said at last.

"Well, yes, as a matter of fact, we do," I said.

"Where?"

"Well, the whole third floor's still unoccupied. The painters are just finishing it off."

"Which room can I have?"

"You mean you want a job?"

"I want peace and quiet and space to work."

"You understand, sir, that the only kind of work that can be done here has to be related to demonology?"

"A perfectly delightful idea."

I looked out into the hallway, to make sure Pine wasn't around, and then whispered, "You really think there might be something to it?"

"What right have I got to think otherwise? Can you prove to me that the Devil doesn't exist?"

"Well, I mean—for heaven's sake, nobody with any education believes in—"

Crack! Down came his cane on my kidney-shaped desk. "Until we prove that the Devil doesn't exist, he's as real as that desk."

"Yessir."

"Don't be ashamed of your job, boy! There's as much hope for the world in what's going on here as there is in anything that's going on in any atomic research laboratory. 'Believe in the Devil,' I say, and we'll go on believing in him unless we get better reasons than we've got for not believing in him. *That's* science!"

"Yessir."

And off he went down the hall to arouse the others, and then up to the third floor to choose his laboratory, and to tell the painters to concentrate on it, that it had to be ready by the next morning.

I trailed him upstairs with a job application form. "Sir," I said, "would you mind filling this out, please?"

He took it without looking at it, and wadded it into his coat pocket, which I saw was bulging like a saddle-bag with crumpled documents of one sort and another. He never did fill out the application, but created an administrative nightmare by simply moving in.

"Now, sir, about salary," I said, "how much would you want?"

He waved the question aside impatiently. "I'm here to do research, not keep the books."

A year later, *The First Annual Report of the Pine Institute* was published. The chief accomplishment seemed to be that $6,000,000 of Pine's money had been put back into circulation. The press of the Western World called it the funniest book of the year, and reprinted passages that proved it. The Communist press called it the gloomiest book of the year, and devoted columns to the tale of the American billionaire who was trying to make direct contact with the Devil in order to increase his profits.

Dr. Tarbell was untroubled. "We are now at the point at

which the physical sciences once were with respect to the structure of the atom," he said cheerfully. "We have some ideas that are little more than matters of faith. Perhaps they're laughable, but it's ignorant and unscientific to laugh until we've had some time to experiment."

Lost among the pages and pages of nonsense in the *Report* were three hypotheses suggested by Dr. Tarbell:

That, since many cases of mental illness were cured by electric shock treatment, the Devil might find electricity unpleasant; that, since many mild cases of mental illness were cured by lengthy discussions of personal pasts, the Devil might be repelled by endless talk of sex and child-hood; that the Devil, if he existed, seemingly took posses-sion of people with varying degrees of tenacity—that he could be talked out of some patients, could be shocked out of others, and that he couldn't be driven out of some without the patients' being killed in the process.

I was present when a newspaper reporter quizzed Tar-bell about these hypotheses. "Are you kidding?" said the reporter.

"If you mean that I offer these ideas in a playful spirit, yes."

"Then you think they're hokum?"

"Stick to the word 'playful,'" said Dr. Tarbell. "And, if you'll investigate the history of science, my dear boy, I think you'll find that most of the really big ideas have come from intelligent playfulness. All the sober, thin-lipped concentration is really just a matter of tidying up around the fringes of the big ideas."

But the world preferred the word "hokum." And, in time, there were laughable pictures to go with the laughable stories from Verdigris. One was of a man wearing a headset that kept a small electric current going through his head, that was supposed to make him an uncomfortable resting place for the Devil. The current was said to be imperceptible, but I tried on one of the headsets, and found the sensation extremely unpleasant. Another photogenic experiment, I recall, was of a mildly deranged person talking about her past while under a huge glass bell-jar, which, it was hoped, might catch some detectable substance of the Devil, who was theoretically being evicted bit by bit. And on and on the picture possibilities went, each seemingly more absurd and expensive than the last.

And then came what I called *Operation Rat-hole*. Because of it, Pine was obliged to look at his bank balance for the first time in years. And what he saw sent him prospecting for new oilfields. Because of the frightful expense involved, I opposed the undertaking. But, over my objections, Dr. Tarbell convinced Pine that the only way to test Devil theories was to experiment with a large group of people. Operation Rat-hole, then, was an attempt to make Nowata, Craig, Ottawa, Delaware, Adair, Cherokee, Wagoner, and Rogers counties

Devil-free. As a check, Mayes County, in the midst of the others, was to be left unprotected.

In the first four counties, 97,000 of the headsets were passed out, to be worn, for a consideration, night and day. In the last four, centers were set up where persons were to come in, for a consideration, at least twice a week to talk their hearts out about their pasts. I turned over management of these centers to an assistant. I couldn't bear the places, where the air was forever filled with self-pity and the dullest laments imaginable.

Three years leter, Dr. Tarbell handed Jessie L. Pine a confidential progress report on the experiments, and then went to the hospital with a case of exhaustion. He had made the report tentative, had warned Pine not to show it to anyone until more work—much more—had been done.

It came as a terrible shock to Tarbell when, on the radio in his hospital room, he heard an announcer introduce Pine on a coast-to-coast network, and he heard Pine say, after an incoherent preamble:

"Ain't been a person possessed by the Devil in these here eight counties we been protecting. Plenty of old cases, but ain't no new ones, 'cept five that was tongue-tied and seventeen that let their batteries go dead. Meanwhile, smack spang in the middle, we let the Mayes County folks take care of theirselves the best they could, and they been goin' to hell regular as ever. . . .

"Trouble with the world is and always has been the Devil," concluded Pine. "Well, we done run him out of northeastern Oklahoma, 'cept for Mayes County, and I figure we can run him out of there, too, and clean off the face of the earth. Bible says there's gonna be a great battle 'tween good and evil by and by. Near's I can figure, this here's it."

"The old fool!" cried Tarbell. "My Lord, *now* what's going to happen?"

Pine couldn't have chosen another instant in history when his announcement would have set off a more explosive response. Consider the times: the world, as though by some malevolent magic, had been divided into hostile halves, and had begun a series of moves and countermoves that could only, it seemed, end in disaster. Nobody knew what to do. The fate of humanity seemed out of the control of human beings. Every day was filled with desperate helplessness, and with worse news than that of the day before.

Then, from Verdigris, Oklahoma, came the announcement that the trouble with the world was that the Devil was at large. And with the announcement came an offer of proof and a suggested solution!

The sigh of relief that went up from the earth must have been heard in other galaxies. The trouble with the world wasn't the Russians or the Americans or the Chinese or the British or the scientists or the generals or the financiers or the politicians, or, praise be to God, human beings anywhere, poor things. People were all right, and decent and innocent and smart, and it was the Devil who was making their good-hearted enterprises go sour. Every human being's self-respect increased a thousand-fold, and no one, save the Devil, lost face.

Politicians of all lands rushed to the microphones to declare themselves as being against the Devil. Editorial pages everywhere took the same fearless stand—against the Devil. Nobody was for him.

In the United Nations, the small nations introduced a resolution to the effect that the big nations all join hands, like the affectionate children they really were at heart, and chase their only enemy, the Devil, away from earth forever.

For many months following Pine's announcement, it was almost necessary to boil a grandmother or run berserk with a battle-axe in an orphanage to qualify for space on the front page of a newspaper. All the news was about Armageddon. Men who had entertained their readers with whimsical accounts of the Verdigris activities became, overnight, sober specialists in such matters as Bratpuhrian Devil-gongs, the efficacy of crosses on bootsoles, the Black Mass, and allied lore. The mails were jammed as badly as at Christmastime with letters to the U.N., Government officials, and the Pine Institute. Almost everybody, apparently, had known all along that the Devil was the trouble with everything. Many said they'd seen him, and almost all of them had pretty good ideas for getting rid of him.

Those who thought the whole thing was crazy found

themselves in the position of a burial insurance salesman at a birthday party, and most of them shrugged and kept their mouths shut. Those who didn't keep their mouths shut weren't noticed anyway.

Among the doubters was Dr. Gorman Tarbell. "Good heavens," he said ruefully, "we don't know what we've proved in the experiments. They were just a beginning. It's years too soon to say whether we were doing a job on the Devil or what. Now Pine's got everybody all whooped up to thinking all we have to do is turn on a couple of gadgets or something, and earth'll be Eden again." Nobody listened.

Pine, who was bankrupt anyway, turned over the Institute to the U.N., and UNDICO, the United Nations Demonological Investigating Commitee, was formed. Dr. Tarbell and I were named as American delegates to the Committee, which held its first meeting in Verdigris. I was elected Chairman, and, as you might expect, I was subjected to a lot of poor jokes about my being the perfect man for the job because of my name.

It was very depressing for the Committee to have so much expected—demanded, even—of them, and to have so little knowledge with which to work. Our mandate from the people of the world wasn't to prevent mental illness, but to eliminate the Devil. Bit by bit, however, and under terrific pressure, we mapped a plan, drawn up, for the most part, by Dr. Tarbell.

"We can't promise anything," he said. "All we can do is take this opportunity for world-wide experiments. The whole thing is assumptions, so it won't hurt anything to assume a few things more. Let's assume that the Devil is like an epidemic disease, and go to work on him accordingly. Maybe, if we make it impossible for him to find a comfortable place in anybody anywhere, he'll disappear or die or go to some other planet, or whatever it is the Devil does, if there is a Devil."

We estimated that to equip every man, woman, and child with one of the electric headsets would cost about $20,000,000,000, and about $70,000,000,000 more a year for batteries. As modern wars go, the price was about right. But we soon found that people weren't inclined to go that high for anything less than killing each other.

The Tower of Babel technique, then, seemed the more practical. Talk is cheap. Hence, UNDICO's first recommendation was that centers be set up all over the world, and that people everywhere be encouraged in one way or another, according to native methods of coercion—an easy buck, or a bayonet, or fear of damnation—to come regularly to these centers to unburden themselves about childhood and sex.

Response to this first recommendation, this first sign that UNDICO was really going to go after the Devil in a businesslike fashion, revealed a deep undercurrent of uneasiness in the flood of enthusiasm. There was hedging on the part of many leaders, and vague objections were raised in fuzzy terms like "running counter to our great national heritage for which our forefathers sacrificed unflinchingly at . . ." No one was imprudent enough to want to seem a protector of the Devil, but, all the same, the kind of caution recommended by many in high places bore a strong resemblance to complete inaction.

At first, Dr. Tarbell thought the reaction was due to fear—fear of the Devil's retaliation for the war we wanted to make on him. Later, after he'd had time to study the opposition's membership and statements, he said gleefully, "By golly, they think we've got a chance. And they're all scared stiff they won't have a chance of being so much as a dogcatcher if the Devil isn't at large in the populace."

But, as I said, we felt that we had less than a chance in a trillion of changing the world much more than one whit. Thanks to an accident and the undercurrent of opposition, the odds soon jumped to an octillion to one.

Shortly after the Committee's first recommendation, the accident happened. "Any fool knows the quick and easy way to get rid of the Devil," whispered one American delegate to another one in the U.N. General Assembly. "Nothing to it. Just blow him to hell in his headquarters in the Kremlin." He couldn't have been more mistaken in thinking the microphone before him was dead.

His comment was carried over the public address system,

and was dutifully translated into fourteen languages. The Russian delegation walked out, and telegraphed home for a suitable reaction. Two hours later, they were back with a statement:

"The people of the Union of Soviet Socialist Republics hereby withdraw all support of the United Nations Demonological Investigating Committee as being an internal affair of the United States of America. Russian scientists are in full agreement with the findings of the Pine Institute as to the presence of the Devil throughout the United States. Using the same experimental techniques, these scientists have found no signs whatsoever of the Devil's activities within the boundaries of the U.S.S.R., and, hence, consider the problem as being uniquely American. The people of the U.S.S.R. wish the people of the United States of America success in their difficult enterprise, that they may all the sooner be ready for full membership in the family of friendly nations."

In America, the instant reaction was to declare that any effort on UNDICO's part in this country would mean a further propaganda victory for Russia. Other nations followed suit, declaring themselves to be already Devil-free. And that was that for UNDICO. Frankly, I was relieved and delighted. UNDICO was beginning to look like a real headache.

That was that for the Pine Institute, too, for Pine was dead broke, and had no choice but to close the doors at Verdigris. When the closing was announced, the hundreds of phonies who'd found wealth and relaxation in Verdigris stormed my office, and I fled to Dr. Tarbell's laboratory.

He was lighting his cigar with a hot soldering iron when I entered. He nodded, and squinted through the cigar smoke at the dispossessed demonologists milling around in the courtyard below. "About time we got rid of the staff so we could get some work done."

"We're canned, too, you know."

"Right now I don't need money," said Tarbell. "Need electricity."

"Hurry up, then—the last check I sent the Power and Light Company was as rubber as your overshoes. What is that thing you're working on, anyway?"

He soldered a connection to the copper drum, which was about four feet high and six feet in diameter, and had a lid on the top. "Going to be the first M.I.T. alumnus to go over Niagara Falls in a barrel. Think there's a living in it?"

"Seriously."

"Such a sober boy. First read me something aloud. That book there—see the bookmark?"

The book was a classic in the field of magic, Sir James George Frazer's *The Golden Bough*. I opened it to the bookmark, and found a passage underlined, the passage describing the Mass of Saint Sécaire, or the Black Mass. I read it aloud:

"'The Mass of Saint Sécaire may be said only in a ruined or deserted church, where owls mope and hoot, where bats flit in the gloaming, where gypsies lodge of nights, and where toads squat under the desecrated altar. Thither the bad priest comes by night . . . and at the first stroke of eleven he begins to mumble the mass backwards, and ends just as the clocks are knelling the midnight hour. . . . The host he blesses is black and has three points; he consecrates no wine, but instead he drinks the water of a well into which the body of an unbaptized infant has been flung. He makes the sign of the cross, but it is on the ground and with his left foot. And many other things he does which no good Christian could look upon without being struck blind and deaf and dumb for the rest of his life.' Phew!" I said.

"Supposed to bring the Devil like a fire alarm box brings the hook-and-ladder," said Dr. Tarbell.

"Surely you don't think it'd really work?"

He shrugged. "I haven't tried." The lights suddenly went out. "That's that," he sighed, and laid down the soldering iron. "Well, there's nothing more we can do here. Let's go out and find an unbaptized infant."

"Won't you tell me what the drum is for?"

"Perfectly self-evident. It's a Devil-trap, of course."

"Naturally." I smiled uncertainly, and backed away from it. "And you're going to bait it with Devil's-food cake."

"One of the major theories to come out of the Pine Institute, my boy, is that the Devil is completely indifferent to Devil's-food cake. However, we're sure he's anything but indifferent to electricity, and, if we could pay the light bill, we could make electricity flow through the walls and lid of this drum. So, all we have to do, once the Devil is inside, is to throw the switch and we've got him. Maybe. Who knows? Who was ever crazy enough to try it? But first, as the recipe for rabbit stew goes, catch your rabbit."

I'd hoped I'd seen the end of demonology for a while, and was looking forward to moving on to other things. But Dr. Tarbell's tenacity inspired me to stay with him, to see where his "intelligent playfulness" would lead next.

And, six weeks later, Dr. Tarbell and I, pulling the copper drum along on a cart, and laying wire from a spool on my back, were picking our way down a hillside at night, down to the floor of the Mohawk Valley, in sight of the lights of Schenectady.

Between us and the river, catching the full moon's image and casting it into our eyes, was an abandoned segment of the old Erie Ship Canal, now useless, replaced by channels dredged in the river, filled with still, brackish water. Beside it lay the foundations of an old hotel, that had once served the bargemen and travelers on the now forgotten ditch.

And beside the foundations was a roofless frame church.

The old steeple was silhouetted against the night sky, resolute, indomitable, in a parish of rot and ghosts. As we entered the church, a tugboat pulling barges somewhere up the river sounded its horn, and the voice came to us, echoing through the architecture of the valley, funereal, grave.

An owl hooted, and a bat whirred over our heads. Dr. Tarbell rolled the drum to a spot before the altar. I connected the wires I'd been stringing to a switch, and connected the switch, through twenty feet more of wire, to the drum. The other end of the line was hooked into the circuits of a farmhouse on the hillside.

"What time is it?" whispered Dr. Tarbell.

"Five of eleven."

"Good," he said weakly. We were both scared stiff. "Now listen, I don't think anything at all's going to happen, but, if it does—I mean to us—I've left a letter at the farmhouse."

"That makes two of us," I said. I seized his arm. "Look—what say we call it off," I pleaded. "If there really is a Devil, and we keep trying to corner him, he's sure to turn on us—and there's no telling what he'd do!"

"You don't have to stay," said Tarbell. "I could work the switch, I guess."

"You're determined to go through with it?"

"Terrified as I am," he said.

I sighed heavily. "All right. God help you. I'll man the switch."

"O.K.," he said, smiling wanly, "put on your protective headset, and let's go."

The bells in a steeple clock in Schenectady started striking eleven.

Dr. Tarbell swallowed, stepped to the altar, brushed aside a squatting toad, and began the grisly ceremony.

He had spent weeks reading up on his role and practicing it, while I had gone in search of a proper site and the grim props. I hadn't found a well in which an unbaptized infant had been flung, but I'd found other items in the same category that seemed gruesome enough to be satisfactory substitutes in the eyes of the most depraved demon.

Now, in the name of science and humanity, Dr. Tarbell put his whole heart into the performance of the Mass of Saint Sécaire, doing, with a look of horror on his face, what no good Christian could look upon without being struck blind and deaf and dumb.

I somehow survived with my senses, and sighed with relief as the clock in Schenectady knelled twelve.

"Appear, Satan!" shouted Dr. Tarbell as the clock struck. "Hear your servants, Lord of Night, and appear!"

The clock struck for the last time, and Dr. Tarbell slumped against the altar, exhausted. He straightened up after a moment, shrugged, and smiled. "What the hell," he said, "you never know until you try." He took off his headset.

I picked up a screwdriver, preparing to disconnect the wires. "And that, I hope, really winds up UNDICO and the Pine Institute," I said.

"Well, still got a few more ideas," said Dr. Tarbell. And then he howled.

I looked up to see him wide-eyed, leering, trembling all over. He was trying to say something, but all that came out was a strangled gurgle.

Then began the most fantastic struggle any man will ever see. Dozens of artists have tried to paint the picture, but, bulging as they paint Tarbell's eyes, red as they paint his face, knotted as they paint his muscles, they can't recapture a splinter of the heroism of Armageddon.

Tarbell dropped to his knees, and, as though straining against chains held by a giant, he began to inch toward the copper drum. Sweat soaked his clothes, and he could only pant and grunt. Time and again, as he would pause to catch his breath, he was pulled back by invisible forces. And again he would rise to his knees, and toil forward over the lost ground and inches beyond.

At last he reached the drum, stood with stupendous effort, as though lifting bricks, and tumbled into the opening. I could hear him scratching against the insulation inside, and his breathing was amplified in the chamber, awing.

I was stupefied, unable to believe or understand what I'd seen, or to know what to do next.

"Now!" cried Dr. Tarbell from within the drum. His hand appeared for a moment, pulled the lid shut, and once more he cried, sounding far away and weak, "Now."

And then I understood, and began to quake, and a wave of nausea passed over me. I understood what it was he wanted me to do, what he was asking with the last fragment of his soul that was being consumed by the Devil in him.

So I locked the lid from the outside, and I closed the switch.

Thank heaven Schenectady was nearby. I telephoned a professor of electrical engineering from Union College, and, inside of three-quarters of an hour, he had devised and installed a crude air-lock, through which air and food and water could be gotten to Dr. Tarbell, but which always kept an electrified, Devil-proof barrier between him and the outside.

Certainly the most heartbreaking aspect of the tragic victory over the Devil is the deterioration of Dr. Tarbell's mind. There is nothing left of that splendid instrument. Instead, there is something that uses his voice and body, that wheedles and tries to gain sympathy and freedom by shouting, among other bitter lies, that Tarbell was dumped into the drum by me. If I may say so, my own role has not been without pain and sacrifice.

Since the Tarbell affair is, alas, controversial, and since, for propaganda reasons, our country cannot officially admit that the Devil was caught here, the Tarbell Protective Foundation is without Government subsidies. The expense of maintaining the Devil-trap and its contents has been borne by donations from public-spirited individuals like yourself.

The expenditures and proposed expenditures of the Foundation are extremely modest in proportion to value received by all humanity. We have done no more in the way of improving the physical plant than seemed absolutely necessary. The church has been roofed and painted and insulated and fenced in, and rotting timbers have been replaced by sound ones, and a heating system and an auxiliary generating system have been installed. You will agree that all of these items are essential.

However, despite the limits we have placed on our spending, the Foundation finds that its treasury is badly depleted by the inroads of inflation. What we had laid aside for small improvements has been absorbed in bare maintenance. The Foundation employs a skeleton staff of three paid caretakers, who work in shifts around the clock, feeding Dr. Tarbell, keeping away thrill-seekers, and maintaining the vital electrical equipment. This staff cannot be cut without inviting the incomparable disaster of Armageddon's victory's turning to defeat in a single, unguarded instant. The directors, myself included, serve without compensation.

Because there is a larger need, beyond mere maintenance, we must go in search of new friends. That is why I am writing to you. Dr. Tarbell's immediate quarters have been enlarged since those first nightmarish months in the drum, and now comprise a copper-walled, insulated chamber eight feet in diameter and six feet high. But this is, you will admit, a poor home for what remains of Dr. Tarbell. We have hopes of being able, through open hearts and hands such as yours, to expand his quarters to include a small study, bedroom, and bath. And recent research indicates that there is every hope of giving him a current-carrying picture window, though the cost will be great.

But whatever the cost, we can make no sacrifices in scale with what Dr. Tarbell has done for us. And, if the contributions from new friends like you are great enough, we hope, in addition to expanding Dr. Tarbell's quarters, to be able to erect a suitable monument outside the church, bearing his likeness and the immortal words he wrote in a letter hours before he vanquished the Devil:

"If I have succeeded tonight, then the Devil is no longer among men. I can do no more. Now, if others will rid the earth of vanity, ignorance, and want, mankind can live happily ever after.—Dr. Gorman Tarbell."

No contribution is too small.

Respectfully yours,
Dr. Lucifer J. Mephisto
Chairman of the Board

WHERE DO I GET MY IDEAS FROM?
YOU MIGHT AS WELL HAVE ASKED
THAT OF BEETHOVEN. HE WAS
GOOFING AROUND IN GERMANY
LIKE EVERYBODY ELSE, AND
ALL OF A SUDDEN THIS STUFF
CAME GUSHING OUT OF HIM.
IT WAS MUSIC.
I WAS GOOFING AROUND LIKE
EVERYBODY ELSE IN INDIANA,
AND ALL OF A SUDDEN STUFF
CAME GUSHING OUT. IT WAS
DISGUST WITH CIVILIZATION.

1/58

List of Illustrations

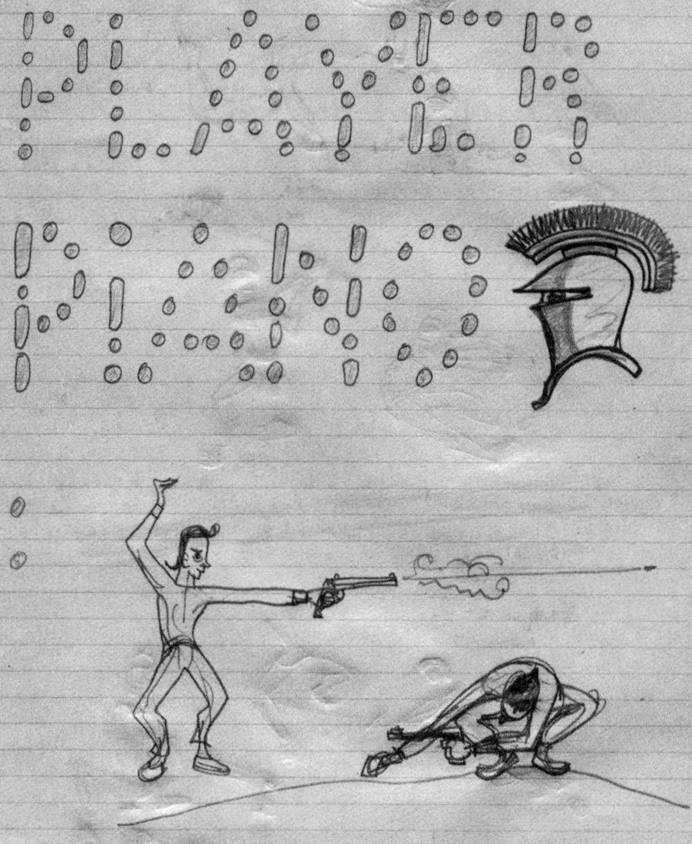
PLAYER
PIANO